SCHOOL RESOURCE OFFICER:

FUNCTIONING AS A COP IN TODAY'S HIGH SCHOOL

School Resource Officer: Functioning as a Cop in Today's High School

By

Detective Mark Walerysiak, former SRO
Meriden Police Department
Meriden, Connecticut

Copyright © 2005 by Mark Walerysiak

All rights reserved.

No part of this book may be reproduced or transmitted in any form or by any means, electronic or mechanical, including photocopying or recording, or by any information storage and retrieval system, without written permission of Mark Walerysiak.

ISBN 1-4116-3652-X

Cover design by Michael Dagata. Visit http://photobucket.com/albums/v283/Helzon to see more of Mr. Dagata's artwork.

Any product names mentioned herein are trademarks of their respective owners.

For Michelle

Contents

INTRODUCTION IX

BECOMING AN SRO 1

SETTING UP 17

THE FIRST DAY OF SCHOOL 25

THE FIRST YEAR OF SCHOOL 50

SCHOOL CRIMES 76

SERIOUS INCIDENTS 104

ALLIES OF THE SRO 118

TOOLS OF THE TRADE 143

SUMMER 154

NEW FACES 163

MAINTAINING THE PROGRAM 170

INDEX 181

Introduction

I'm guessing that if you're reading my introduction then you're either one of those people who has to read a book cover to cover, or you really want to know EVERYTHING there is to know about being a school resource officer. In any event, I'm glad you're reading it because it's a way for you to get to know me before our journey into the world of the school police.

As you can tell by the preceding paragraph, this is going to be a casual read. I've been through all those police books that put you to sleep before you get to the table of contents. What good is it to try and learn from the book if the book isn't interesting? Sure, I could write in the third person and produce a typical law enforcement book, but does the world really need another one of those? Have you seen some of the promotional books out there?

I believe that you will have a much more enjoyable and educational experience if I present information to you in a common sense, laid-back fashion. I also have plenty of stories that I'd like to share with you regarding my experience as a police officer in a public high school, which is why I chose to write this book in the first-person perspective.

My years as a police officer in a high school were some of the most memorable of my career. Although I'm no longer an SRO, I still like to keep in contact with the great many friends that were made at the school. My new position as a detective dealing with juvenile crime is only enhanced by my experience as an SRO.

And so, out of respect for those of you who took the time to read my introduction, I'll conclude it here and hope that the following pages help you attain a better understanding of what it means to be a school resource officer.

Det. Mark Walerysiak

BECOMING AN SRO

Have you ever noticed that there's a book for everything? Really, there are books out there on almost every conceivable subject. And I'm glad there are. In 2001, I had taken a promotional exam for sergeant at the Meriden Police Department in Meriden, CT, and thanks to several law enforcement books I was able to study and obtain a respectable score. The books on criminal investigation, search and seizure, community policing, and police supervision were very helpful in preparing me for the exam.

During the time of the exam, I was a school resource officer for one of the area high schools. A short time after the examination I began thinking, "What if one day our department requires an examination for the position of school resource officer?" I hadn't recalled seeing any books on the subject. Before you could say "dot.com," I went to Amazon's web site and several other online booksellers. I typed in the subject "school resource officer" and watched as my monitor displayed that there were no matches for that phrase. "Well that's not very fair," I thought to myself. I realized that the SRO position was catching on across the country and was a relatively new concept, but I was amazed that I could not find one book on the subject.

Well my friends, that's why I chose to write this book. It is my firm belief that the school resource officer position is not only here to stay, but that it will continue to grow across the country as well. The reason for that belief will be found in the following pages.

Keep in mind that some names were changed to protect the innocent, so to speak. However, even though some names are changed, the stories are real. So let's delve into this peculiar position of law enforcement and find out more about becoming a school resource officer.

*   *   *

Who among us has not seen the TV show Cops? Almost everyone has. In fact, that show was one of the contributing factors which led me to want to become a police officer. I loved watching the police get into their exciting police chases and responding to shots-fired calls. My adrenaline would pump every time I saw a suspect fighting with an officer, resulting in all the back-up officers running to the rescue. I loved it. And I knew that's what I wanted to do. Helping people. Working outdoors. Getting the bad guys off the streets. That's what it's all about, right? Of course it is. And I've had my share of all of the above. No doubt about it, being a police officer is one of the most exciting jobs around.

I remember my rookie year thinking, "I wonder where I'll end up here? How far up the ladder will I go? Maybe a captain? I'd love to be a detective too."

Fast-forward four years from my date of hire. I'm assigned to one of two public high schools in the city of Meriden, CT. Orville H. Platt High School to be exact. I was one of four new school resource officers assigned to a specific school. The second high school in the city also acquired an SRO, as did the two middle schools. This position took me off the streets, locked me in the same building for eight hours a day, and gave me the responsibility of curtailing any criminal activity among one-thousand hormonal teenagers. Oh, and by the way, I requested the position.

When I was still on patrol and the memo came out asking for interested officers to sign up for the city's first ever SRO program, I was very hesitant. This was a totally new position which no one was sure how to perform. We had no reference point and it was uncharted territory. Initially, and I'm being brutally honest here, I was interested in the position because the schedule was a dream. At the time, I was rotating to a different shift every two months. That's not something one's body is fond of doing. When I learned that the SRO position was Monday through Friday from 7:00 a.m.-3:00 p.m. (weekends off!), I couldn't help but consider it.

But then I started thinking of the downside. "What if I start, and end up not liking it? What if the students drive me crazy? What EXACTLY does it entail?" I had a big decision on my hands.

I talked it over with my wife Michelle and some fellow officers. Everyone seemed to think it would be the right move for me. So after several weeks of pros and cons, I made my decision to throw my hat into the ring.

Depending on the agency, the selection process for any position varies. In Meriden, the police department and personnel department decided to hold interviews for the SRO candidates. The interview panel consisted of Lt. John Thorp, who would be the SRO supervisor; the personnel director; each school's respective principal; a school resource officer from Manchester, CT; and a DARE officer.

Now, my police department has 130 officers. How many do you think signed up for the newly created SRO positions? Twenty? Thirty? Try six. That's right, six. Now I wasn't all too confident signing up in the first place. How do you think I felt when I found out there were six willing participants? Suddenly I felt like a lab rat walking into an experiment that was going to go haywire. In any event, I prepared myself for the interview and walked into the conference room at City Hall and answered the questions to the best of my ability. For my interview, the principal of Platt High School was not available so I only dealt with the other four panelists.

I felt confident walking out of the room and was actually anticipating the results. What I didn't anticipate was not being selected. Since I had the second-least amount of time on the force compared with the other interviewees, I wasn't too surprised that I wasn't chosen. Disappointed? Yes. Surprised? No.

Fate, however, is a funny thing. A few days later, I was in the police station when I ran in to Lt. Thorp, the SRO supervisor. He was standing with one of the captains. "Hey, Mark," said Thorp. "Are you still interested in the SRO position?" My eyes lit up. "Absolutely," I responded. Thorp went on to explain that one of the candidates' wives was pregnant and that a permanent day shift would not be accommodating to his schedule. Just like that I was assigned to Platt High School.

And that's how I became a school resource officer.

*   *   *

Now let's get one thing straight right off the bat. Being an SRO is not for everyone, and not everybody can do the job. I'm not saying this to be a braggart; I'm just stating fact. To this day I have fellow officers come up to me and ask me how I was able to put up with all those kids day in and day out. My brothers in blue told me they wouldn't become an SRO under any circumstances. Ever. They openly admit that it takes a different kind of personality to work as a cop in a school. Read that sentence again. The key word there, boys and girls, is "personality." Before the interview, before the training, before the actual placement in the school, you need to know whether or not you have the personality and demeanor to deal with teenagers on a constant basis.

Fortunately, I have a very flexible personality and can get along with anyone. I don't know why that is or how it came to be, but you've got to be a rare individual if I can't carry on a conversation with you. At the very least, I pretend that I'm interested in what you have to say. That may sound a bit harsh, but it's a perfect example of how a school resource officer needs to act at times. Think about it. If you're assigned to a public high school and you're dealing with a thousand different teenage personalities as well as a hundred different teachers, do you honestly think that you can survive by acting the same towards everyone? One student may be shy, and you need to know how to approach him. Another may be a wise guy and give you a hard time. There's no way you can talk to these two individuals in the same manner, especially if you're going to be in contact with them on a daily basis. You might be able to get away with it on patrol since you may never see the person you're dealing with again. But in a school, where you're permanently assigned, your initial impressions with the students—and even the faculty—are crucial.

So the very first thing to think about when considering an SRO position is how flexible your personality is. The other three officers who were selected as SROs along with me exhibit flexible personalities. And it is because of this trait that they were successful in their positions. I shudder to think what some officers would be like in a high school setting. Not only would they be kicked out of the school within a week, but there would probably be several internal affairs complaints lodged against the officer because he/she is just incapable of demonstrating any type of decorum.

It's a difficult thing knowing that, as a police officer, you have arrest powers and can determine the fate of people's lives, yet you must use constant restraint and not overstep your boundaries at the school level. As an SRO, you are still a police officer, but you are not the boss. The principal is in charge of the school and what he says is the way it is. If you're not able to accept that then you won't last long in a school. Yes, on several occasions a police officer can exceed a principal's authority over a school, but those instances are rare. For the most part, an SRO is there to assist the principal and his school and to function as a valuable RESOURCE.

A flexible personality is crucial. Do you have it? Are you okay with kids calling you by your first name, or do you demand to be called "Officer?" Will you have a problem with the school principal telling you how things are going to be done, or do you have a problem from taking orders from someone who is not even your boss? What will your reaction be when you hear a student tell you that he won't stand for the Pledge of Allegiance and that war veterans aren't worth his time? Will you be able to control your temper?

Those are just a few examples that I encountered in my first week at Platt High School. Each one of them required a flexible personality.

I don't believe someone can be taught to have a flexible personality. You either have one or you don't. If an officer is thinking of becoming an SRO and feels that he'll be able to adapt after getting the position, then that officer is in for a rude awakening. Besides, if you're not sure whether you have the right personality or not, just look at your past record as a police officer. Did you get along with most of your coworkers? How many complaints did the public file against you? If the answers to those two questions are "no" and "a lot," respectively, then maybe the SRO path is not for you. Just a hunch.

*   *   *

Okay, so you've got the personality. It's flexible. You get along with mostly everyone and you feel that SRO is the way to go. (No I didn't mean for that to rhyme.)

SCHOOL RESOURCE OFFICER: FUNCTIONING AS A COP IN TODAY'S HIGH SCHOOL

What's the next step? Well, now you have to let your supervisors know that you're interested in the position. That's pretty self-explanatory, right? Either sign up on a sheet like I did or tell your supervisor directly or do whatever it is that your department requires of you when a new position becomes available. But what makes a supervisor choose one officer over another when deciding on an SRO? I'm going to take the high road here and avoid the subject of politics and cronyism because I know some of you are thinking that. Besides, we've already touched on one of the desirable traits: a flexible personality. But we don't want to overlook the obvious. A police officer who has any type of experience dealing with children in some capacity definitely has an upper hand when it comes time for supervisors and principals to decide on which cop they want in their schools.

As I've stated earlier, I was one of four SROs selected for the new school resource officer program. Out of the four, I am the only one who had no real previous experience dealing with children. (Does having once been a kid count?) The other three SROs all had not just some, but a good deal of experience with kids. And since I'm going to mention my three SRO pals throughout this book, I might as well introduce them now before I go any further.

I'll start with Officer Kristin Muir. Kristin came on the job a few months after I did and the two of us immediately hit it off. Her previous work experience includes working with mentally retarded adults for six and a half years. Working with these mentally handicapped people was, in essence, the same as dealing with children. They had childlike needs and characteristics that Kristin was able to confront. Obviously this was one of the reasons why she was a natural choice for the SRO position. Throw in the fact that she has a bachelor's degree in child psychology and you've got yourself a model SRO. Being a female didn't hurt either. Kristin was assigned to a middle school, and children at that age level probably feel much more comfortable dealing with a female police officer rather than a male officer.

Lincoln Middle School, where Kristin was assigned, is directly across the street from Platt High School. This close proximity of our respective schools and the fact that Kristin and I had a good friendship helped the two of us to team up and work together to combat any problems we saw in (or around) the schools. Specific examples of such plans will appear later in the book.

The two remaining SROs were assigned to schools on the east side of Meriden. Officer Mike Lane was assigned to a middle school and Officer Sal Nesci was assigned to a high school. Lane was a natural pick for school resource officer because he was involved with police Explorers for the past twelve years. For the uninitiated, the Explorers is a national program for youths between the ages of fourteen and twenty-one. It introduces adolescents to the reality of police work. Details of the program include riding along with police officers on their tours of duty, attending a week-long academy, shooting at a range, holding weekly meetings, and other fun activities. Officer Lane's leadership role as Head Advisor in the Explorer program gave him a clear advantage in dealing with young students at the middle school level. Lane's background is exactly the type of experience that the police department was looking for in an SRO.

Officer Sal Nesci was a D.A.R.E. officer before he became an SRO. This, too, was a major reason why he was selected—aside from the fact that he was a very good officer. As you probably know, D.A.R.E. (Drug Abuse Resistance Education) is a program aimed at warning young children about the harmful effects of drugs and alcohol. Thus, Nesci's experience with interacting and dealing with the youth of Meriden also made his assignment as an SRO a no-brainer. Officer Kristin Muir also was a D.A.R.E. officer before her appointment to Lincoln Middle School. These facts no doubt had a positive impact on deciding whether they would be worthy SROs or not. *But Mark had no experience!*

As stated earlier, my police department required an oral interview for the school resource officer position. Each department is different. Some may just assign an officer with no interview at all. Some may actually test for the position. Like everything else, it varies from location to location. *[consistancy]* The oral interview for the Meriden Police Department lasted about five to ten minutes per candidate. Again, keep in mind that only six officers (including myself) were willing to try the newly created position, so the interviews were over before noon.

Now for the trade secrets. "Mark," you're saying to yourself, "just what kind of questions were you asked in your interview?" Well let me tell you. Nothing too surprising. The questions were pretty much common sense inquiries related to the SRO position and I'm sure you would expect these types of questions. First I was asked how I would handle a problem of students constantly walking in the roadway after school. As time would later show, this is a problem that Kristin and I would battle frequently. But at the time of the interview, I answered that I would constantly patrol the streets in question and warn students to stay on the sidewalk as mandated by law. If the students continued walking in the road in the days that followed, I would be forced to issue them infractions.

10

And if they were too young to be issued tickets, I would either have a talk with their parents or even assign the parent the infraction.

As it turns out, this is exactly what Officer Muir and I did after school on a daily basis. And it worked beautifully. More on Operation: Sidewalk later.

Another question asked of me during the interview: What would I do if a female student approached me and told me that she had a crush on me and wanted to have a relationship? Trying to impart a bit of humor into the interview, I replied that I would tell the student that I was happily married. Since I heard nothing but crickets in the background I immediately followed up with my serious answer which was to tell the student that her comment was very inappropriate and that we would have to go to the office and speak with an administrator regarding the matter. As an SRO, I would not want to simply end the discussion with the female student without at least letting a member of the school staff witness the dialogue I have with her.

Boards of education take the preceding situation very seriously. In fact, many boards of education initially do not want any officers in their schools, and that is one of the reasons why. Some members of the board feel that certain officers might not be able to control themselves if met with an eager young student. Although this is an unfair sentiment (shouldn't teachers also be carefully scrutinized?), it nevertheless was one that needed to be addressed.

During the interviews of the candidates, the principals were present to give their input to Lt. Thorn on who they thought was the right "man" for the job. Because of scheduling conflicts, there was no principal in the room during my interview. However, the next question I was asked pertained to the principal, and I regard it as the most important question of the interview. I was asked what I thought my role at the school should be and how it will integrate with the principal and his/her duties. My answer was straightforward and honest. "My role at the school is to assist the principal and the administration in any way possible and to be a resource for the school, its students, and the faculty. The principal is the 'captain of the ship' and I am simply there to make sure that the ship runs smoothly, and to deal with any criminal matters that may occur."

Why do I feel that is the most important question in the interview? Because the interviewers want to know how you're going to relate with the principal on a daily basis. Everyone wants to hear that you understand who the man in charge is. It's the principal's school and he is the boss. As mentioned earlier, an officer who comes into the school on the first day with aspirations of doing things his way and changing the school in a direction he sees fit will find himself running radar on the outskirts of town the next day. This point cannot be stressed enough. Don't even apply for the SRO position if you can't get used to the fact that it's the principal's show. How effective can an SRO be if he is constantly overstepping his boundaries or disagreeing with the principal over school matters? That would be like the principal lecturing you on criminal law or telling you if you have enough probable cause to arrest someone. And what kind of principal would want an SRO who is always butting heads with him over issues? A comfortable working relationship between principal and SRO is essential. When these two powerful positions work together, the outcome can only better the school environment and lead to a promising future.

Additional questions to expect in an oral interview for the school resource officer position include the "generic" questions:

- Why are you the best candidate for the job?
- What are your concerns with children in the city?
- Why are you interested in the position?

When encountered with these inquiries, you must answer from your heart and hope that you are saying what the interviewers want to hear. After all, they are generalized questions that, in essence, require the candidate's opinion.

Then there are the more specific types of questions. An excellent web site to find such queries can be found at www.nasro.org. NASRO stands for the National Association of School Resource Officers, of which I am a proud member. They have an excellent web site and address all types of issues related to the SRO program. They also include sample interview questions for the SRO position. I list a few of them here:

- With the high profile cases we have seen over the past few years (in which young people obtained firearms and brought them to school), how do you feel the SRO program can reduce school violence?
- School Resource Officers will typically become involved in what has become known as the TRIAD (Teaching, Counseling, Law Enforcement) concept of school based policing. Which do you feel is the most important part of this TRIAD and why?
- What might make you resign your position as an SRO?

- How would you address a teacher who has just received a traffic violation from one of your fellow officers. The teacher is upset and asking for your assistance in "handling" the ticket for them. What can you do to assist them?
- Within your first week on the job, you are walking through the halls of your school. A student who you have never met makes a derogatory remark directed to you as a Law Enforcement Officer (i.e.: pig) in front of several other students. How do you respond if at all?

These are only a handful of the questions that are listed on the web site. All the questions, in my opinion, are very good and should be reviewed before any oral interview for the position of SRO. Although there are many other aspects of an oral interview that can be addressed, this book is not meant to help you with interviews. There are plenty of works available dealing with that subject.

The questions asked of me and the other candidates in the interviews were direct and to the point. The keys to remember are to use common sense, remember that the principal is the boss (with a few exceptions), and the SRO is at the school to assist in every capacity that a police officer can. Keeping these points in mind will help you when it's time to answer the many types of questions that will be thrown your way.

*   *   *

So we've covered the *who* and the *how* aspects of becoming a school resource officer. But what about the *why*? Sounds simple enough. Why do you want to be an SRO? Is it a burning desire to help the youth of America? Are you burnt out from patrol duties? Is it because you have a thing for teachers? What exactly is your reason?

I'm going to give you an answer that is unconventional and—some might say—controversial. My answer is this: IT DOESN'T MATTER. That's right, read it again. It does not matter why you want to be an SRO. Go back and read the suggestions I just listed. Let's take them one by one. Why do you want to be an SRO? "Is it a burning desire to help the youth of America?" If you answered "yes," well then God bless you and I hope you succeed. "Are you burnt out from patrol duties?" If you answered "yes," then I hope this new position invigorates you. "Is it because you have a thing for teachers?" If so, then I wish you luck in your relationships. <u>Now although your answer doesn't matter, what DOES matter is that when you become an SRO, you do the absolute best job your ability allows.</u>

Think about it. If you're a cop right now, does your supervisor care about why you became a police officer, or is he more concerned with your work and productivity? That's what I thought. The same goes for any position. As long as your work is fruitful, nobody cares about why you got there. They just want to know how you're doing now.

I'm a perfect example. Want to know why I wanted to be a school resource officer? The schedule. Prior to becoming an SRO, I was rotating shifts around the clock every two months. Any cop can attest that the body was not meant to stay up all night. Two months on first shift, then two months on second shift, and then two more on third shift. It's enough to do quite a number on your body. After several years of doing that, I now had the opportunity to work a steady day shift from 7:00 a.m. to 3:00 p.m., Monday through Friday. Are you kidding me? Steady days with weekends off?! Where do I sign?

Please don't think I was the only one who applied for the position because of the schedule. It's just human nature to do what's best for yourself. Some liked the schedule; some were just sick of working patrol day after day. Are these selfish reasons? Maybe. Did they affect any of our job performances? Not at all. Work ethic is the key.

It's amazing what a good work ethic will do. But in many occupations, you really don't have a choice. Police work is one of those occupations. If you get transferred to another division and your work is not up to par with everyone else's, you'll get transferred back to where you were just as easily. I've seen it in my department and I'm sure it's happened in others.

If your work ethic stands on its own merit, then that is all that matters. Why should it matter why I want the job? All that should matter is that the job gets done in an efficient and professional manner. So don't be embarrassed to tell people why you really want the position (except for the interviewers...unfortunately, you still must tell them what they want to hear). After all, many people in this world take new positions because of the salary alone. In Meriden, the SRO position pays the same as a patrolman's position. But like I said, each department does its own thing.

So congratulations! You got the position! Buckle your seat belt and hang on while I tell you what to expect during your first few weeks in the school....now that the easy part is behind you.

SETTING UP

In Connecticut, school begins during the last week of August or the first week of September, depending in which city you live. If you've just been selected as a school's new resource officer, your department should have arranged a meeting with you and the school's administrators prior to the start of the school year. The meeting does not have to be lengthy. Rather, it should just cover the basics. For example, this is when you get to actually sit down and "feel out" the principal (and believe me, he's doing the same thing to you). The same goes for the assistant principals, if there are any. Platt High School has two assistant principals along with the head principal.

After introductions and friendly discourse, the SRO and administrators should at the very least lay a groundwork of what is expected of the officer and how he should work with the administrative staff. Although this is important to discuss early on, one must remember that this will be a learning process. Situations will occur throughout the school year where you will learn more of what the administrative staff expects and how they react to certain incidents.

Besides the introductions and discussions of expectation, an obvious tour of the school is in order. Get to know your school building. Every inch of it. Being a school resource officer at Platt High School, I knew that I was in charge of the entire building's security. Become very familiar with the school's head custodian. Find out where everything is located. This includes water, gas, and electrical shut-off valves; entrances to the roof and basement; closets; crawl spaces; and storage areas. Nothing is more embarrassing than being assigned to the school for months (or even years) and not knowing where a place is located in the building. When you're first assigned to the school you'll have ample time to walk around and examine all the nooks and crannies. It's amazing how students can find their way into the most obscure places. And in a school environment, not only is that likely, but it can also become dangerous. Know your school well and monitor its areas frequently.

During the tour of your new school, you'll likely come across some of the teachers that work there. Here's where your flexible personality comes into play. Be friendly with as many teachers as possible. Undoubtedly you're going to come across some members of the faculty who aren't very congenial or, worse yet, don't like the police. Do not let this dissuade you. For four years I talked to a faculty member of the high school who, through her hints and innuendoes, appeared to not care for cops. However, she got along with me fine. Contradictory? Maybe. But this just proves that if you make an effort to work at the school relationships, you'll be seen as the person you are rather than just "the school cop."

I was very lucky in my school because I didn't have problems with any teachers. I honestly liked all of them and had the greatest amount of respect for what they did each day. I would often tell them that I could never do their job, and although they would say the same thing about my profession, I still felt that they had the more difficult job.

The initial meeting with the school's administration is also an ideal time to ask about communications. Most high schools now use radios or "walkie-talkies" as a means of transmitting any messages. If the school you become assigned to does not have a radio system, you will find yourself at a great disadvantage. When instant communication is needed for a fight or other emergency, the radio system becomes an invaluable tool. Strongly suggest to your principal, supervisor, and board of education that a radio system be utilized in the school. It will improve response time, facilitate all communications, and allow for better coordination. I can't imagine what my job would have been like without a school radio. On any given day I could be anywhere in the building. Suddenly, I would hear the receptionist call on the radio that a fight was occurring in front of Room 138. Immediately, I would run to the area and help break up the fracas with nearby teachers.

Another example involves afternoon dismissal. During this time, I stayed in front of the school by the street, crossing students and directing buses out of the driveway. The principal would stay at the corner of the school 40 yards away. He would keep an eye on the students walking home and alert me to any problems he saw.

Without a radio, I would never be able to hear him, and if he were to walk over to me and inform me of the situation, the incident would have either ended or escalated. If you haven't figured it out by now, what I'm trying to say is....get a school radio. Although it is possible to function as an SRO without one, you will become more efficient in every way by adding a radio to your equipment.

Let me make clear at this point that I realize you can't always get what you want. Although I was fortunate to have a school radio, I was not as blessed when it came to securing an office for myself. Allow me to spend some time on this issue.

When the SRO program first evolved in Meriden, the Board of Education did not agree on how it should be implemented. The issue of offices came up and the superintendent immediately shot it down. You see, her philosophy was that we should not be stationed in the schools, but rather in the community around the school. If the school should need us, she felt that we would be in the area and able to respond quickly. Now I know that I'm not a superintendent of schools (nor do I wish to be one) but I was a school resource officer, and let me just say that that philosophy is wrong. When I speak later about the importance of building rapport with students, I will discuss how to accomplish it as well as the benefits it provides. It does not take an Einstein to realize that rapport cannot be established between an SRO and a student if the officer is stationed outside of the building. But the Board of Education could not get past the badge, handcuffs, and pistol, and believed that if the officers were stationed in the building, then the school would be like prison camp. This, of course, is just ignorant thinking, as I have made more friends of parents, teachers, and students than I ever imagined possible. This is because I am not stationed in the community, but in the school. I really have no choice. During my first few days in the position, I tried to stay out of the school but I soon realized the absurdity of it all because as soon as I left the building, I would be called back inside again to help with an incident. So eventually I just parked my car in the lot and stayed in the school. The principal, however, would not budge on the office issue. And I don't blame him at all. After all, the superintendent is his boss and he shouldn't defy her wishes. So where would I stay you ask? I would learn to use different rooms of the school at different times. Sometimes I would put myself in the back room of the upstairs library. Other times I would use the first- or second-floor faculty lounges. There was a private conference room next to the principal's office that I frequently used. And on occasion I would even use an empty classroom.

Although I was able to endure this constant movement, I never stopped hoping for an office to come my way. There would be several instances where a student would want to talk to me about a personal issue and I would bring him into the conference room. After a minute or two, an administrator or faculty member would come in and say they needed the room because a meeting was scheduled at that time or because they needed a larger room. So the student and I would move to an empty assistant principal's office. Now both assistant principals were very nice and allowed me to use their offices at any time, but when I saw them start heading toward their offices, I would pull the student out yet again and move to a third room. I probably didn't have to move, but I know that I would get a little annoyed if someone was in my chair when I needed to be in it. After all, it is the assistant principal's office, not mine. And it wasn't his fault that I didn't have my own place.

This type of foolishness in playing "musical rooms" was very distracting and, in my opinion, unprofessional.

Phone calls are another issue. For those of us who are police officers, we know that we frequently make confidential calls to parents or to other police agencies. There were times when I needed to make immediate, private calls, but could only get to a phone that might as well have been in the middle of Times Square. I would have teachers and sometimes even students walking by me while I was discussing a private matter on the telephone.

Another reason that SROs should have offices is accessibility. Many times when students—or even teachers—wanted to find me they had to go to the main office, ask for me, have the school secretary page me, and wait several minutes for me while I worked my way to the office. An SRO with his own office can always be readily available. Within a matter of days the students and faculty would all know where the SRO's office is located and would feel comfortable knowing that their conversation will be private.

Do not underestimate the power of your board of education. As you can see in my example, it can single-handedly affect the focus of the SRO program. I can't help but laugh when I recall the semiannual meetings the SROs would hold with the school principals and superintendent. The Meriden School Superintendent would often say that she believed the Meriden SRO program was the model program and the most professional in the state. Yet she refused to allow offices for these "model" SROs for fear that the public would perceive the schools in a negative light. Many SROs that I know in other cities throughout Connecticut, as well as throughout the country, are housed in schools not only with offices, but computers, Internet access, and many other tools that help facilitate the task of a school resource officer. This type of cooperation between the school system and the police department is essential in building a "model" SRO program.

Obviously when you first meet with your administrators you don't want to demand an office. That wouldn't be a great way to start the working relationship. I recommend you do what is expected, and in time your work will be appreciated and the staff will recognize what you need to continue as a successful SRO. Heck, it took me two years just to get a file cabinet so that I could stop piling things up in a corner where I kept my reports and other materials.

*   *   *

Before your first school year actually begins, see if you can obtain keys to the building. Hopefully your school will be secure from intruders, meaning most doors—if not all—should be locked during the school day. As an SRO, I was leaving and entering the school building on a frequent basis. Obviously, having keys to get into the school from any entrance made my exits and returns easier. I also recommend getting keys for as many interior doors as possible. A master key would be ideal, but if separate keys are the only option, don't hesitate to take them. School resource officers need to have as much access to the school as possible. How else can we be expected to monitor certain rooms or areas? The more access you have to the school, the more ability you will have to prevent or discover a crime.

A school resource officer may also find it beneficial to become familiar with the school's alarm system, if it has one. I've met several SROs at conferences and workshops who've told me that they not only have the alarm code to their school, but that they also respond as key holders when the alarm activates after school hours. Obviously distance plays a part in this scenario, but many SROs live relatively close to their respective schools, which would enable the above situation to occur.

So you've done everything your supposed to do. You've met the administrators, you've set up your office, and you've received your school radio, keys, and alarm code. You're ready to meet this new challenge head on. You're ready to start your new position and you've got the motivation to go with it. After putting in years of patrol or community policing, you believe that you can take on anything. But can anything prepare you for the one thing that will change your life? Can anything prepare you for.......high school students?

THE FIRST DAY OF SCHOOL

Now the real fun begins. It's the first day of school. You woke up for work and it feels a bit odd that you're not going on patrol today, shagging calls for eight hours. No, instead you'll be in a public high school meeting a thousand new faces. Congratulations.

Of course each experience is going to be different. It depends on many factors: school size, municipality, staff personalities, school economy, student backgrounds, and a host of others. But let me just give you, the reader, a little taste of what it was like on my first day of school. I'd wager that many other SROs have experienced similar conditions.

I arrived at Platt High School at 7:15 a.m. I drove into the front lot with other cars as parents were dropping off their children to the front door of the school. I watched the cars turning in from the main road and noticed that traffic was beginning to back up on said road. What's an officer to do? I immediately took action and began directing traffic from the road into the school. Three days later I stopped doing morning traffic. I quickly learned that I was only making the traffic problem worse because of the design of the road and its intersection with the school entrance. I left the cars alone and, although minor buildup occasionally occurred, the traffic was fine. So much for making a big impression on the first day.

7:35 a.m. The homeroom bell rings. I pick up my school radio and meet the office clerical staff. A great bunch of ladies. Six new names for me to learn. Now it's crucial that you become close with your school's clerical staff. They will be a priceless asset to helping you start out and they can provide you with a wealth of information on students.

7:41 a.m. Homeroom ends and the students enter the hallways and change classes. The only way to describe this event is to have you picture everyone at Disney World getting off the rides at the same time and flooding out to the walking areas. It was an absolute nightmare, especially since I was convinced to throw myself into the fray and immerse myself in the student body as soon as possible.

Now let me remind you that I was Platt High School's first school resource officer. So what do you think the reaction of students would be when they see a fully uniformed, armed police officer walking in the halls as they are changing classes? I don't believe I've ever had that many eyes on me in my entire life. I heard students whisper about me. Laugh at me. Point at me. Avoid me. It was very uncomfortable. This type of behavior lasted for about two weeks. After that, the students became used to me and realized that I wasn't going away. But those initial two weeks were almost unbearable.

It was during these class changes that I got to see the students in their natural surroundings. I wasn't prepared for what I saw and heard. Some high school students have a very vulgar vocabulary and this became evident as I was walking the hallways. Be prepared to hear every obscene word that exists. During my tenure, I even heard some vulgarities that were new to me.

Besides the language, you'll notice that many students dress a bit inappropriately. Most high schools do have a dress code that basically states that clothing cannot be distracting or disruptive to the learning process. However, "distracting or disruptive" is a very subjective expression. I've seen some teachers send students to the office for clothing they felt was too risqué, only to have the administrators send the student back to class, overruling the teachers initial referral. This type of subjectivity causes many students to slip through the cracks and get away with wearing extremely provocative or inappropriate clothing. Be prepared to see boys with pants hanging almost down to their knees. Girls with skirts that give new meaning to the word "mini." Then you'll notice the hairstyles and colors. It's enough to have a police officer run for the door.

I observed all this within a four-minute time span while the students changed classes. I quickly learned to love the sound of the bell signaling the beginning of class. The halls became empty and everything was peaceful again.

Okay, so now it was 7:45 a.m. on my first day of school. What do I do now? I took a walk around the building to make sure all the doors were secured and then returned to the main office. The ladies in the office were busy at their desks and everyone knew what they were supposed to be doing. Everyone but me. So I decided to go out to my police cruiser and run some radar on the road adjacent to the school. The school would call me if they needed me and I would be seconds away. After stopping a couple of vehicles I came to the conclusion that my traffic enforcement could be seen from the classroom windows and was probably a distraction to the students inside. I packed up and moved to the empty school parking lot that was located across the street from the school and just sat in my cruiser wondering what to do next and if this new position was really a good idea.

Again, this was something that I did for a couple of weeks until the school began to utilize me more frequently. For those first few days I would just sit in my police cruiser and try to think of some way to get involved with the school.

As I sat in the parking lot on that first day, I saw a student walk out of the building and down the street. I thought I should officially meet my first student, and I drove over to him. Wouldn't you know my luck? I had just found a freshman skipping school. On the first day yet! I talked to the youngster and told him he had to be in school since he was under sixteen years of age. I let him know that his only other alternative was to be brought to the police station and picked up by a parent. Needless to say, I gave him a ride back to school.

So I had performed by first intervention as an SRO and I was very proud of my accomplishment. The student was brought to the office where he was dealt with by one of the assistant principals. I then left the office and made another round of door checks and headed back out to my cruiser. Again, I didn't know what to do next. I couldn't call my partner, Officer Kristin Muir, who was assigned across the street at Lincoln Middle School. She could not come to work that day and would be in the next morning.

I decided to go back inside and meet more people. Since classes were in session, I introduced myself to some of the custodians. Five more names to learn. They were a great bunch of people and welcomed me to the school. I can't tell you what a relief it was to be welcomed by the staff. Each time a new staff member gladly received me I felt another weight lifted off my back. After all, I'm a stranger in a new land. Not only that, but I'm a police officer and people have different opinions about cops.

Several teachers also came across my path as I was walking in the building. Naturally, I forgot their names as soon as they told them to me because I was still trying to remember the clerical workers' and custodians' names. However, I made a concerted effort to put my memory into overdrive and remember as many names as possible. In general, people seem to be a bit friendlier when you remember their names and address them accordingly. It's much better than saying, "Hi, you," or "Hi, pal," or just "Hello."

Finally 11:00 a.m. rolled around. This was the beginning of a 75-minute lunch period that was divided into three waves. Nothing prepared me for what I was about to see. The lunch bell rang and all the students on the first lunch wave came down and went into the cafeteria. What I didn't expect was that when the students finished eating, they were allowed to congregate in the main corridor outside the cafeteria. Within a matter of minutes, there were hundreds of students gathered in the corridor laughing, joking and doing anything else they felt like doing. I seemed to be in a setting of controlled chaos. Most police officers will agree that

29

when a large crowd forms the situation becomes uncomfortable. Too often I've been involved in circumstances where crowds become unruly or violent and a mob mentality sets in. That is not an enjoyable experience, and seeing three-hundred students milling around in a hallway with very little supervision was not my idea of a good time. Nevertheless, I remembered that I did not make the rules in the building and that I was new to the environment. I decided to suppress my concerns for now and concentrate on the task at hand which entailed introducing myself to the students. What better time than now when they're all together and in a relaxed state?

Before I describe how I went about talking to students, you must understand that there are two types of people. Some people are naturally outgoing and always ready to talk to someone. Their interactions with strangers are effortless and often result in a positive rapport with the person. The other type of person is usually quiet and reserved. He usually has to make an effort to be personable and would sometimes rather be left alone. I hesitate to use the terms extrovert/introvert only because I feel they are too labeling in nature. In any event, you would think (and rightly so) that school resource officers should fit under the former classification. However, I fall under the latter category. Again, I would not call myself an introvert, but I am slightly reserved and do not freely begin conversations with strangers. Once I become acquainted with someone or feel I can trust that person as a friend I then become very personable and almost appear to be an extrovert. You can see, then, that I had my work cut out for me, as would any SRO in my position. Not being one who usually initiates contact, I

THE FIRST DAY OF SCHOOL

now found myself walking up to strange teenagers and asking them if they saw the latest *NSYNC video or Tony Hawk skateboard.

High school teenagers are a unique sort. I don't know if there is a more diverse age group than teenagers. One moment I can be talking to a preppy tennis player wearing a Polo shirt and Dockers, and if I continue down the school hallway I'll next find myself conversing with a girl dressed in jet black who will proclaim to me the benefits of the Wicca religion. Yet these were the types of students that I somehow needed to connect with. <u>As an SRO, the goal is to actually form a bond with the students so that they can trust you and rely on you for any help or concerns they may have.</u>

So on my first day of school I knew in my mind that I would get nowhere in this position unless I could befriend as many students as possible. They are the ones who will make you love or hate your time at the school. They are the ones who will give you information if they feel you are trustworthy. Without a doubt, they are the most important relationship you will have at the school.

While I'm on the subject of students, let me just point out that although I've called them "teenagers" and "kids" in my writing, when I speak with a student or group of students and I need to refer to them, I make sure to use the term "student." Think about it. When you were in high school didn't you think you knew everything and that you were pretty much an adult? How did you feel when someone called you a "kid," or "teenager?" I distinctly remember hating those terms. Let me give a quick example. <u>I call Johnny into the office because the principal has asked me to speak to him about banging on lockers during class change;</u>

[handwritten note: → not law enforcement / school rules]

31

WRONG WAY

"Johnny, the principal asked me to talk to you about banging on the lockers in the hallway. He doesn't like when kids walk around the corridors and make unnecessary noises. "

This is a very basic example. But take a look at how two minor alterations can change the overall tone of the discussion.

RIGHT WAY

"John, the principal asked me to talk to you about banging on the lockers in the hallway. He doesn't like when students walk around the corridors and make unnecessary noises."

Don't call him Johnny—unless he asks you to. Johnny gives the impression of a little kid, and if you want to subliminally gain points with this student (not kid), you should treat him with the respect he hopes to get.

This treatment toward students comes in handy when you first meet them. Back on that first day of school I made it a priority to get to know these high school students. I simply walked up to a group of male students that were gathered in the lunch wave hall and started talking with them. The subject is irrelevant as long as it's something they can relate to. For example, I'm not going to talk to them about the rising overtime costs of the police department, but I will mention the local professional baseball team or the latest single by Eminem.

Initially, the students probably thought I was crazy. I mean, here's this fully uniformed cop coming up to a bunch of high school students and talking to them about Slim Shady. Even I felt a little strange doing it. But the importance of such interaction cannot be emphasized enough. I knew that I'd be with these students for at least the next few years and building a relationship with them was key.

So I continued introducing myself on that first day of school, and I was amazed at how smoothly it was going. I was so desperate at wanting to form a bond with these teens that I even told them to forget the formalities and to call me by my first name, Mark. At first I didn't know if that was a good idea, but it turns out to have worked very well. To this day, most of the former students call me Officer Mark (as do the staff, since my last name is horrendous). But back on the first day, I wanted the students to know that I wasn't just another cop. Although I would still enforce the law when needed, I was also assigned to the school to help the students.

During the initial meetings with the students, I made it a priority to memorize their first names, just as I had done with the faculty. And the best way to test your memory is to address a specific student by what you think his name is. I can't tell you how many times I called a student by his wrong name, but I can tell you that it was much less than the names I got right. Besides, for the names you screw up, don't fret. Students are very forgiving and are flattered that you're taking time out to speak to them.

On that first day of school I probably spoke to 25 students. Of those, I think I remembered ten names. But if you keep up the process day after day, you'd be amazed at the amount of students you get to know. By the end of that first day of school, I had two of the students I met say good-bye to me. One said, "Good-bye, Officer Mark," and the other said, "Later, Mark." To me, that indicated my first day was successful.

* * *

When I talked about radios in the last chapter, I made reference to my school dismissal traffic duties. This part of the day is only comparable with when students change classes in between periods. In fact, dismissal is even worse. All the students are happy to be out of school all the while looking for their friends and not really caring about school rules at that point. Almost all the students passed by me since I was right in the front doing hand traffic and crossing students.

Be prepared for the first time you hear a school dismissal bell ring. The exodus of students is very intimidating at first. After all, it's your first day as an SRO and you've got 1,000 kids coming toward you. There are voices coming from all different directions, some of them not so kind. For several weeks, I dreaded dismissal traffic duties. Many fights broke out after school; students old enough to drive would "peel out" of the parking lot; smoking on school grounds continued after school. And then there are the parents who disregard the school buses' flashing red lights. Don't even get me started on that one.

Would you believe me if I told you that within a matter of months, I actually looked forward to dismissal time? How is that possible, you're asking yourself? Throw in one cup of interest, two cups of humor, a dash of wit, and a sprinkle of helpfulness, and you've got yourself a recipe for a successful traffic duty.

While I stood out there in front of the school directing traffic in those opening weeks, I knew that I'd be blowing a huge opportunity if I didn't build rapport with the students during that critical time. The school day is over, the students are relaxed and in a better mood, and many of them are together in one place. I realized this was a key time and place to play "Officer Friendly." The following is a demonstration of how an introductory conversation would take place between a student and myself. Keep in mind that this was the way I'd speak to students anywhere I met them, not just after school.

Me: "What's up, pal? How's everything goin'?"
Student: "Good."
Me: "Hey, I just want to let you know that you're gonna be seeing a lot of me here at the school. I'm the new school resource officer here and if you need me for anything don't hesitate to ask, OK?"
Student: "OK."
Me: "Cool. You could call me Mark or Officer Mark, whatever you want. We don't have to be formal since we're gonna see each other everyday. I didn't get your name."
Student: "Darryl."
Me: "Alright, Darryl. Nice to meet you, man. Remember, if you need anything, come to the main office and ask for me."
Student: "Alright, man."
Me: "Later."

And that's it. I would do this dozens of times a day until I became more comfortable with the student population. As an SRO, you have to talk on the student's level. You can't conduct a conversation with them the way you talk to a complainant on patrol.

"Nice to meet you, sir. If you have any concerns with your fellow students or any criminal activity that may affect you in any way, please notify me so that I can rectify the situation in an expeditious manner."

Are you kidding me? You'd be laughed out of the school faster than a substitute teacher wearing a bow tie. It's imperative that you talk to the students the way that they talk. If you're talking to a student who's a wannabe gang member, you're going to have to talk in his lingo so that you two are "straight." Of course, I don't want you to have an entire conversation in street talk. Professionalism is still a priority. But you can't talk to him the way you talk to the principal or your lieutenant. Use your judgment. Throw in some words so that this guy knows you understand him. It's okay to say "straight" for "all right" or "boys" for "friends." This type of verbal rapport has proved very successful for me and even more so for Officer Sal Nesci who is the other high school SRO across town. He takes verbal rapport to an art form and as a result is extremely well liked by the student body.

The subject of rapport building can be a book in itself. Without a doubt, rapport is, in my opinion, the single most important aspect of a successful SRO program. I may mention other factors that are very significant or "one of the most important aspects," but I can make a definite stand that rapport is the key to the program.

Let's think about patrol for a bit. I'm going on the assumption that most of the people reading this book have some type of police experience, which hopefully includes patrolling. After all, can you be a real cop if you haven't patrolled the streets for a few years?

Not likely. Now what does patrol entail? Going from call to call and solving problems for people that you usually are not going to meet again. Yeah, sure, there a few houses that you just always keep going back to. But for the most part, you never see most of the people you deal with ever again. Not so with a school resource officer. In fact, in a way, being an SRO is completely opposite from being a patrolman. As an SRO you see the same group of people day in and day out. Many of these people that you see (students, teachers, etc.) actually become your friends. How many friends' homes have you responded to while on patrol?

Another way that being an SRO differs from patrol duties is that normally, when you're on patrol, once your shift is over, that's it. You're done. As an SRO you carry school problems for days and weeks on end. Billy and Jose might have major problems with each other everyday and you know that a fight is going to break out despite constant mediations. No matter what happens you know that you're going to have to talk to both of them again down the road. Not only that, but it's your responsibility to come up with a solution for the two boys. This is where building rapport becomes so important. I actually had students at the school that trusted me more than any other faculty member. Some of the students would rather talk to me than any other person, including their friends. I'm not stating this to gloat, rather, I'm trying to point out that my rapport with these students led them to actually trust me in matters that were usually personal to them.

So how does one build rapport with a high school teenager? Well, I've already described the introductory phase. But obviously that is not enough. Let's use our pal Darryl whom we referred to a couple of pages ago when I introduced myself to him at the school's dismissal. The first step, which may seem easy enough, is to remember Darryl's name. How many people can you build rapport with if you don't know their names? The next step would be to constantly address Darryl when you see him in school, whether it be in the hallways, cafeteria, dismissal, or even anywhere outside of school. I'm also very touchy with the students and usually have some kind of physical contact with them. I know what you're thinking and we'll discuss that subject in a later chapter. I usually shake the student's hand, "high-five them," or put my hand on their shoulder. It's a much more personal contact and really focuses their attention on you. Eventually, if I have enough contact with Darryl, he's going to know that I am a permanent fixture at the school and that I can be student-friendly when need be. The trust will begin to grow.

The next step is not always necessary, but when used it is practically foolproof. There will come a time when Darryl will do something that may violate school rules. For example, I may see Darryl in the hallway without a pass, or I may catch him smoking in the bathroom. If the violation is minor enough, I may tell Darryl that I am giving him his one "get out of jail free card" and that I'll keep the violation between the two of us. However, I will add that he now "owes me one" and that if he ever breaks that same rule again, I will come down hard on him as will the school administration. I cannot emphasize enough how well this tactic works. It succeeds on two fronts. First, the student believes that you are the best cop in the world because you just let him get away with something he wasn't supposed to be doing. And second, he will fulfill his end of the bargain and give you something in return. That something could be as simple as not giving you a hard time the next time you tell him to do something. Or it could be as major as telling you what student is walking around the school with a knife in his pocket. Whatever the circumstance, Darryl will not forget what you did for him and will return the favor. One example I immediately recall involved a student named George. This student was known as a troublemaker and frequently gave the faculty a hard time. However, I had excellent rapport with George and we would even joke around with each other at times. One day the office secretary called for the assistant principal, Greg Shugrue, and myself to respond to a teacher's room for a student who refused to leave. When Mr. Shugrue and I arrived at the classroom, we saw that George was the insubordinate student. Although he refused to leave for the teacher, George needed little more than a look of disappointment on my face and he reluctantly got up and came with Mr. Shugrue and me to the main office.

Sure, you may be thinking, "Well you're a cop, of course he's going to go with you." Let me assure you that is not always the case, especially involving students with whom I do not have rapport. Yes, it's true. Not all the students will turn out to be your friend and some of them will test you to your limits. In my first year as SRO there was a student at the school named Steven. He was a very disruptive student from a terrible home life. He was one of those students that you knew would spend the rest of his life in jail. Drugs, fighting, and causing trouble were the only subjects this fifteen-year-old was passing. It was the middle of the year and I had already arrested Steven once for disorderly conduct. Nevertheless, I still tried building rapport with him and tried forming some type of connection with him. But there are just some students who won't take. Steven was one of them. Although he

39

would give me a "what's up" every now and then, he had no interest in having any kind of bond with the enemy, which in his case was the police department.

This one day, Steven had just been suspended for the umpteenth time and was to leave school grounds. For some reason he became very loud and belligerent to Joseph Paluszewski, Platt's other assistant principal who had just suspended Steven. I was down the hallway and saw Steven in the main corridor yelling and swearing. I approached him and told him to quiet down and to leave the building. Steven just ignored me and seemed to yell and swear even more. At that point I grabbed him by the arm to place him under arrest for disorderly conduct (he was very loud and disrupting nearby classrooms). To my surprise, Steven pulled away from me and started to confront me. I pushed Steven chest first into a wall to get some kind of control over him and then handcuffed him as quickly as possible. He continued creating a disturbance even as I walked him out to my police cruiser in the front parking lot. This was one case where rapport was just not possible. Oh, and just for the record, Steven did not attend Platt High School much more after that incident. In fact, as of this writing, I believe he is in jail.

That example brings up a fascinating point. You've just read about one of the many arrests I've made at the school. Now let me explain how rapport relates to making those arrests. Again, we see here a difference between patrol and SRO. In patrol work, you make the arrest, process the arrestee, and go on to the next call, likely to never see that person again. When you're assigned to a school and end up making an arrest there, you're going to see the person you arrested on the following day. Now isn't that a nice and

40

THE FIRST DAY OF SCHOOL

comfortable feeling for you? But if you have the proper rapport with the student, it really isn't that bad. I've honestly had students come up to me on the day after I arrested them and shake my hand or ask me how I'm doing. They understand that I have a job to do and that they made a mistake. It's analogous to a parent grounding a child. The parent and child see each other everyday and have a close relationship with each other, but there may be times when the parent has to exert some form of discipline. This is how it is at school with a student and an SRO. But the officer must have that personality which enables the rapport to take place.

The relationships between the students and myself have been so solid that I hardly ever needed to handcuff those students whom I knew well. Making an arrest at the school is, in essence, like arresting your little brother or sister. Obviously there are times when some students, like the aforementioned Steven, are so bad that they need to be cuffed and treated more cautiously. But for the most part, when I knew that an arrest needed to me made, I explained to the student what was happening and what will happen. And as long as the student was calm and cooperative I walked with them to my cruiser and transported them to the police department. This type of scenario would be impossible without good rapport. I would never even *think* of arresting someone on patrol without handcuffing him. But working in a school with students that you know quite well enables the officer to have this type of discretion. And the way you affect an arrest is a type of subliminal rapport building in itself. After all, what would your attitude be toward a police officer who treated you with respect and brought you to the police department without handcuffing you and then bought you a bag of chips from the police vending machine as you waited for your parents to come pick you up. Is it any wonder those students quickly learn to trust you and become amicable toward you?

Good rapport should be the basis of any SRO program. Without it, not only will the officer be unsuccessful, but the school will also not benefit in any way. An SRO without good rapport building is akin to a mute security guard.

*   *   *

If good student rapport is the baseline for a successful program, then gathering information from student informants would have to be the next level. Yes, you read correctly. Student informants exist in schools, and they are a treasure to find. I know what you're thinking. "Informants? This guy thinks he's working *NYPD Blue* or *Homicide: Life on the Streets*." Not exactly. But the informants I got in school were basically motivated by the same reasons as street informants.

In *Criminal Investigation* (seventh edition) by Swanson, Chaemlin, and Territo, informants are categorized into several different types:

- Mercenary informants look for financial reward.
- Rival informants seek to eliminate competitors in criminal activity.
- Plea-bargaining informants are looking to reduce charges against them.
- Anonymous informants are unknown and therefore cannot be accurately judged.

- Legitimate informers are law-abiding citizens looking to help the police.
- Self-aggrandizing informants have much knowledge of criminal activity and feel important sharing information with the police.
- False informants intentionally provide bogus information.
- Fearful informants are worried that they are in danger from a criminal associate and therefore contribute information.

(As a side note, for those of you studying for promotional exams to supervisory or investigator positions, the above-mentioned book is a very good source of study.)

My experience in a public high school has shown me that of the many different types of informants listed, two predominate over all the others. I have found that legitimate informers and self-aggrandizing informants make up most of the high school student informant population. The legitimate student informers I've encountered throughout my years at the high school were usually just your everyday, run-of-the-mill students who felt that it was necessary to tell me the information they had. Most of these students who came forward knew me well, for I had excellent rapport with them. Very rarely would a student with whom I did not often fraternize come forward to me with any criminal information. This fact alone shows just how important the rapport aspect of the SRO program is.

When I began to see that many of my informants were actually legitimate student informers who felt that they needed to do the right thing, I became greatly encouraged. This showed me that many students felt strongly about their school and knew that they were a key asset in my ability to keep the school "clean." They realized that, after Columbine and Paducah and Santana, they needed to act when they became aware of any potentially dangerous students. I would stress this to students whenever I spoke to them in their classes, but the fact that many students were doing it on their own before I even gave my lectures was gratifying in itself.

*   *   *

Working in a high school day after day can be very grinding. Just ask any teacher. I frequently would have to deal with the problem students and I'd often wonder if there were any good kids left out there. This is similar in patrol work where police quickly become cynical and pessimistic because they are constantly dealing with the worst society has to offer. However, when legitimate students came up to me looking for help regarding a situation they felt warranted police action, I quickly learned that—just as in patrol work—not all people are bad. There are a great many students who care for their school and do the right thing when pressure is usually on them to do the opposite. Many students would never dare "rat" on their friends and end up just ignoring the situation. As we know all too well, this kind of thinking can be fatal. As a school resource officer you must keep in mind just how difficult it is for some students to "tell" on others. Peers, media, and even some parents still teach children to not be a "snitch." Fortunately, many students come to the realization that if they don't "snitch" they quite possibly could become another statistic.

In order to ensure that students continue to supply an SRO with valuable information, the officer must be truthful in regards to the way confidentiality will be handled. In Platt High School, I told students that anything they told me would be absolutely confidential and that no one else would ever know they told me. However, I sometimes needed to add that there are exceptions to the rule. For example, whenever I was told of an incident that may have resulted in an arrest, I made it a priority to tell the legitimate informer that I may be forced to disclose his name in a court of law. I also added that the chances of this were very small since very few of my arrests end up in trial. But as far as police reports, or when I spoke with parents (if the child was no longer a juvenile), teachers, or other students, I made sure to keep the student's name anonymous.

Confidentiality is a very delicate subject. On the one hand, you must be sure to keep your word to the student. If I, as an SRO and authority figure, were to ever lie to a student and disclose his/her name as the informer, I would not only risk ever getting classified information again, but I would also damage the student-SRO relationship that I worked so hard to establish. If the student/informer could not trust me with one important piece of information, how could he ever trust me about any other aspect of his life such as his personal or family problems. Worse yet, my actions would be a direct reflection on the police department. This student would believe that the police in general could not be trustworthy.

On the other hand, as a police officer I have a sworn duty to enforce laws and stop crime. If I ever came to the point where I was forced to give the name of a student informer in order to validate the arrest or properly prosecute the crime, I'm not sure what I would do. I might find the informer and ask if it would be okay to divulge his name in order to prosecute the crime. If the student allowed the disclosure I would be all set. But if the student still insisted on remaining anonymous, I would have to weigh my options. Would I feel that the crime of the suspect outweighs the informer's wish to remain nameless? Or is the value of the informant and his future knowledge higher in importance than the suspect's crime? This is dangerous territory and an SRO must weigh his options to figure out which choice will be better for the informer, the school, and himself. Thankfully, this type of scenario has never happened to me, but it is definitely possible. The moral here is to make sure you never, ever promise something that you can't keep. It took months, even years, for me to build rapport with the students at Platt High School. Creating an atmosphere of distrust could wipe out that work in seconds.

Up to this time I have only mentioned one of the two main types of informants I found at Platt High School. While it would be nice to have exclusively legitimate informers because of their high standards and sense of right and wrong, that is not a reality. The other major type of student informant I've encountered is the self-aggrandizing informant. As Swanson, Chamelin, and Territo define the term: "The self-aggrandizing informant has many contacts in criminal circles and feels important by giving information to the police."

Remember now, public high school is not a monastery. Criminal activities do take place there. I don't care if you're attending Beverly Hills High or Detroit High, you're going to find some illegal activity there, just as in any other facet of society. The students who know about this activity because they hang out in some of these "criminal circles" are the ones who will become your self-aggrandizing informants. In my first year as SRO at Platt High

Informants offered heresay which could lead to searches?

THE FIRST DAY OF SCHOOL

School I met a student named "Nick." Nick knew all about what was going on in the school and who the players were. Nick talked like he was a member of the Beastie Boys. He would use words like "phat," and "chillin,"" and "homeboy." He was very street savvy but also seemed to be fake, and initially I wanted nothing to do with him. Then one day Nick came up to me out of the blue and told me that a certain student was carrying some marijuana on his person. Nick told me he personally saw the drugs and I confirmed the student in question by showing Nick a picture of said student's school I.D. card. When I had gathered all the information I needed, I alerted the appropriate assistant principal who then had the authority to make the search. Lo and behold, the drugs were found and shortly thereafter the offending student was arrested and expelled.

In the two years that Nick "worked" with me, his information was wrong only one time. That is an amazing percentage. I grew to actually like Nick and finally asked him why he was helping me. He said that he admired the police and even considered being one, but he realized that chance was slim because of the crowd with which he associated. He added that his real interest lied in the military anyway.

On the day that Nick graduated I realized that I had lost a truly valuable asset. I thanked him for all his help and wished him luck with the rest of his life. I added that if he ever needed anything from the Meriden Police Department that he should not hesitate to contact me. I haven't seen him since.

I cannot stress enough that student informants are a product of rapport. If I had treated Nick the way I wanted to the first time I met him he would never have approached me again. "Hey, Nick,

47

how about paying attention in English class so that you could learn yourself a real vocabulary." A statement even closely resembling that would deter any further contact from Nick.

Your flexible personality is what allows you to build rapport with the students. As I stated earlier, I didn't fit the mold, so I molded myself. A good sense of humor goes a long way when trying to build rapport. Bring yourself back to your days as a student in high school. Then just update that role with today's social pressures. If you're capable of thinking in that mode, you've just made your job as a school resource officer that much easier.

Again, it is important to remember your official capacity as a sworn police officer. But the way you use that capacity to build relationships with students that you will see everyday for the next four years is what will set you apart from an unsuccessful SRO:

- Be friendly with the students, even those that sometimes give you a hard time. I found that students who were usually difficult frequently needed my help at least once in their school career. And if you give them that help, it will change the way they respond to you. They will never forget what you did.
- Go above and beyond what is called of you as an SRO. Students aren't blind. They can tell if you're a lazy cop, or if you're dedicated to your job and diligent. How do you think they pick their favorite teachers?
- Treat the students fairly and with respect. This is key. Many of these students don't know what respect is. Lead by example. This is by no means an easy task and can take

a full four (or even five) years for a student to understand. Some students will never get it. Many will.
- A sense of humor will make rapport building a breeze. Kids love to see a cop that laughs like a human being. Their impression of the police comes from watching TV shows or movies where the cops are all too serious. The students immediately loosen up and open up when they see that you're a "cool" cop.

Remember, rapport building is *the* most important element of an SRO program. If you don't think you're capable of most of what I've just described, you'd be better off responding to those barking dog complaints.

THE FIRST YEAR OF SCHOOL

In the last chapter I discussed my first day of school at Platt High School and the importance of rapport with students. By all means, one day is not enough to give you an insight into the world of a school resource officer. A school year in Meriden, Connecticut, is 180 days long. That's a lot of days. A whole six months. What did I do for that many days at the school? What duties did I have? Did I just hang around and wait for fights to break out? Read on.

*   *   *

In those first months at Platt High, I really wanted to connect with the students. Yes, I know, I already explained rapport building.

But that was on a one-on-one level. I wanted to reach these students en masse. But how could I do that? My initial thought was to have the student body—or at least the newest incoming class—meet with me for a short question answer session in the auditorium. I thought this would be a great way for me to introduce myself to the students and explain to them what I expected of them and how I work. I pictured myself on the stage giving them a short speech:

> "I can be your best friend in this school, or I could be your worst enemy. That decision is up to you and the choices you make."

I pictured myself answering any questions they had and telling them that they could all talk to me whenever they needed me. This, however, was not to be.

Before I go any further, let me get this out of the way. I got along fine with Platt's principal, Tim Gaffney. Tim is an all-around good guy who really does want the best for his school. The two of us have had a positive working relationship and he has been very supportive of my role at the school. However, since I was the new kid on the block, I didn't want to come into the school that first year and ask for too much. I wanted to feel my way through the territory and get to know everyone's personality first. I didn't want to start rocking the boat with unnecessary requests, even though I thought they might be helpful. For this reason I decided not to ask if I could address the students in the auditorium. I also didn't want to put Tim in an uncomfortable position. I knew that Meriden's Superintendent of Schools didn't want us in the schools too much, so I figured my request would be futile anyway.

Keep in mind that not all boards of education are as unsupportive as Meriden's was. Horace C. Wilcox Regional Vocational Technical School is a state-run high school that is about 400 yards south of Platt High. I made periodic checks there with their then-SRO, Trooper Heather Ingala (since it's a state operated school, they were supplied with a state trooper). Tpr. Ingala was a fine SRO who had unlimited support from the school's administration. We both started at our respective schools in the fall of 2000 and I would visit her school to coordinate any information with her since Wilcox and Platt students congregated together quite frequently.

The first time I visited Tpr. Ingala I found that she not only had an office, but also a personal computer with a printer and all the other bells and whistles. I also learned the following year that she was *encouraged* to make a group address to the students in their cafeteria on the first week of school. So you see, my auditorium-address idea wasn't too bad after all.

But I would not quit! And neither should you! I decided to think of another way to address the students in groups. Fortunately I had access to computers in the upstairs library of the school. I did most of my work on a Macintosh instead of a PC because, well, it's the better computer. That's another book.

My idea was to create a sign-up sheet for teachers who wanted me to speak in their classes to explain to the students why, all of a sudden, there was a police officer assigned to their school. I thought it would be a good way for me to introduce myself to not only the students, but the teachers as well.

I printed out the form, and taped it to the counter in the teachers' mailroom where they all go everyday. And then I waited. And waited.

On the following day I eagerly checked the sign-up sheet. No signatures. Not one. I couldn't imagine what had happened. But I persevered and waited again until the following day. When I entered the school building and headed for the mailroom I was praying for one signature. I looked down at the sheet...four signatures! I was ecstatic! From there the snowball effect began. Four more signatures the next day. Then five the day after I actually had to print another sheet to accommodate all the requests. My foot was in the door.

I'll be honest. I don't remember in which teacher's class I first spoke. Actually, I don't think it matters. What I do remember are the questions. First and foremost on everyone's mind, including the teacher's, was the question of why a police officer was assigned to the school. Some students asked, "Do they think we're going to have a school shooting?" Others chimed, "I didn't think this school was that violent." Automatically the students were associating my presence with violent behavior. I knew I had to curb this thinking, and after running into these types of questions two classes in a row, I decided to explain to the students the real meaning of "school resource officer." The students were confusing me with a "school patrol officer" which is not my title.

The next day I was ready for my class presentation. Before I let any of the students ask me anything, I gave them a fifteen-minute introduction speech that I've used in every presentation since that day. The following is my introduction. I believe it summarizes the SRO's duties accurately and I have received positive responses to it. Feel free to use it entirely or any of its parts:

> Many students are wondering why a police officer is assigned to Platt High School. There are a couple reasons. The first reason is that the police department is trying to reach out in a more personal way to the public. We're aware that the only time most people see the police is when something bad happens. For example, when there's a serious car accident, the police respond. When burglars rob your home the police come over. When you or your parents get stopped for speeding, you get pulled over by us. The association is always there. Bad things happen, the police show up. Bad, police, bad, police.
>
> Well the Meriden Police Departmentis trying to change all that. We want you, the students, to see the police not just when something negative occurs, but also when good things happen. We want you to get to know the police. That's why I'm here, so that you could know me on a personal level. For the rest of your high school career you can now say that you know a police officer. And I will always be there to help you for whatever problem you might have. If you're having problems in school, talk to me about them. If it's trouble at home you're having, I'll do my best to help you out there, too. But don't just think you've got to talk to me about problems in your life. All of you are welcome to talk with me about whatever you'd like, whether it's last night's sports scores or the movie you saw last weekend. Whatever it is, my door is always open.

At this point in the speech I would let them know how to best contact me during the school day. This is important because most of the students wouldn't know how to find me unless they saw me walking in the halls. Giving them an invitation of "any time, any day" let's them feel a little more at ease when they come to talk to you. Hardly any students will want to talk with an SRO if they feel the officer may be busy or doesn't want to be bothered.

As much as I like the preceding speech, I like the next one even more. The first speech opens by stating there are "a couple" reasons why police are assigned to schools. Here is the second:

Another reason that it makes sense for police to be in the schools is quite obvious, but often overlooked. But think about this for a second. This school is like a mini-city, isn't it? I mean, you've got the students who resemble the citizens, and the principal is like your mayor. You've got a cafeteria that can be your restaurant, and a nurse's office is like a mini-hospital. There's even a library here. Doesn't it make sense then, to have your own little police department here to take care of any law related issues?

I can't tell you how effective that analogy is. In all the classes I've spoken to, I've never had a student argue with that rationale. To be frank, I can't see why they would. It's a very true statement. I firmly believe that the school is a type of mini-city, and for those who argue that hardly any crime occurs to warrant a full-time police officer, well....I'll see you in a few pages.

The preceding two speeches that you read have worked wonders for me on explaining my position at the school. Of course, I've added several other speeches (such as my role as it relates to Columbine) but these two are what I find to be the most effective. They're just simple ways to introduce yourself to a large group of students. I would go from classroom to classroom saying the same thing. If I ever encountered a class that had some students who had already heard me speak, I would ask them to be patient as I explained myself to those who haven't.

Some of the presentations I made would run only fifteen or twenty minutes and then I would leave because the teacher wanted to go on with his/her lecture. But some teachers were very accommodating and allowed me to stay for the entire class period to answer questions from the students. Certain teachers went so far as to assign homework to their students to prepare for my presentation. The teachers would have the students go home and prepare a question for me to answer.

I actually loved presentations that took the whole class period. Remember, this is still in the opening months of my new position as SRO and for a large portion of the day I was bored. I would wait for something to happen or for someone to call for me. Boy, do I miss those days!

Full-length class presentations promoted dialogue between the students and me. That was, after all, my intention as a school resource officer. I would get a medley of questions, some very good, some just plain stupid. You have to keep in mind that all these students have different educational backgrounds, so not all the questions are going to be intellectual. One student asked me, "Can I shoot your nine?" Referring to my 9mm pistol, the misunderstood youth apparently needed a new prescription for his glasses since I was carrying a .45 caliber pistol. I responded by asking "Norman" if he had taken any gun safety courses to which he responded, "I don't need no courses, yo." I dismissed Norman by telling him that I would not be able to shoot with him because of his amazing shooting ability. I said that, as a police officer, even I need training courses so I would be just embarrassing myself shooting with a professional like him. The other students chuckled in amusement and Norman stayed quiet for the rest of the class.

Don't be afraid to give back what a student throws at you. I've had students who think they're funny come up to me with their pals and start trying to rattle me. One time a group of students approached me during the lunchtime free-for-all. The leader,

"Nelson," came up to me and said, "You don't look so bad to me." Now I was very familiar with this student and could tell right away he was joking with me and just showing off for his friends. But I couldn't let an opportunity like this pass. As I looked down at Nelson—he was much shorter than me—I replied, "I wish I could say what you look like to me, Nelson, but I can't see that far down." Instant respect. Nelson's friends were doubled over in laughter and the leader himself shook my hand and walked away. Sad as it may seem, that type of wit and banter will earn me more respect from Nelson than the badge ever will. That's just the way it is. Our society no longer produces children who automatically succumb to authority. In some cases, it must be earned. And although I don't agree with that, I do whatever it takes to bond with these students.

These types of confrontations will happen during your classroom presentations as well. You must be prepared for those types of students that show off for the rest of the class. If a student tries to embarrass you, it's up to you to turn the tables on him and make him the butt of his own joke. I know some people who may not agree with this method and believe that the student should never be made to feel embarrassed. But I am telling you that if you don't turn the joke around, those students will own you. The SRO will be nothing more than a substitute teacher. Obviously I am not condoning that the student be ridiculed or berated. What I am saying is that the officer cannot just stand by meekly as the students have a laughfest. One or two quick-witted jabs are all it takes and the classroom is yours. No other student will want to venture out into that territory after seeing your display of humor. Again, this undoubtedly will cause the class to like and respect you. The students will see that you are not a dull officer who talks like a robot. You're not another teacher who just lectures and goes home. You are an actual human being that is relating to them on a level that they know and enjoy. Sounds familiar, doesn't it? If you guessed that it sounds like we're talking about a type of rapport....you win! We're constantly striving for rapport. It cannot be stressed enough. The SRO/student relationship (the rapport) is always the ultimate goal.

Not all students are going to give you a hard time during your classroom presentations (or any other time, for that matter). Most have very intelligent and well thought-out questions. On more than one occasion I learned something myself because I didn't know the answer to the question. I've been quizzed on everything from search and seizure (that's a big one) to motor vehicle law. Driving barefoot (yes, you can), to time limits on detaining a suspect (it depends on the circumstance). But no matter how many classes I went into, I was guaranteed to get asked about one thing: the gun.

Ah, yes....the gun.

I don't think a day went by at the school when I didn't hear about it. Whether it was an administrator, a teacher, a custodian, or a student, someone always had a comment about the gun. To be more specific, they always had a comment about my Sig Sauer .45 caliber semiautomatic pistol. It goes without saying (so then why am I saying it?), but having a gun in a school is a touchy subject. It doesn't matter that it's a police officer's weapon. It's still a gun. The students are fixated on it: "Can I hold it?" "Can I shoot it?" "Have you ever been shot?" "Have you ever shot at someone?" "Have you ever killed someone with it?" "Is it loud?" "Is it loaded?" "Why do you have it in school? It got to the point where I needed to create a sort of gun safety speech/presentation. It was nothing fancy or elaborate. It was actually just a five-minute talk that I interwove with my other speeches.

By the way if you're interested in the answers to the above questions, they are, in order: "NO," "NO," "No," "Yes," "No," "Yes," "Yes," and "(see below)."

Before I give you the gun oration that I told the students, let me address the controversial question, "Why do you have it [a gun] in school?" I should tell you right now that I could count on one hand how many students have asked me this, which tells me that a large majority of the students do not have a problem with me carrying a loaded firearm in the building. After all, I am a police officer and it probably would have seemed more awkward to see a cop without a gun than with one. Nevertheless, there are still a small percentage of students (and probably faculty members) who feel uncomfortable being in a building with a loaded gun regardless of who is carrying it.

I was confronted on this issue by one female student who was very concerned and uneasy. I tried to explain to this freshman that she had nothing to worry about because I was highly trained and knew what I was doing. I continued explaining that after recent school shootings nationwide, it would be senseless to place an officer in a school without a gun. She would not buy it. She could not see past the gun, but at the same time she could not give a realistic answer as to what I should do if a student brought a gun to school and started shooting. She suggested the use of my OC (pepper) spray, and the craziness of the idea made me laugh out loud. That type of response just proves that some civilians really have no idea of what police work entails, including the logistics of a lethal encounter.

59

SCHOOL RESOURCE OFFICER: FUNCTIONING AS A COP IN TODAY'S HIGH SCHOOL

The next day I was walking past the principal's office and I saw Mr. Gaffney talking to this same girl. Apparently she went to him with her concern because when I walked by I heard him trying to explain to her why it was important to have an armed officer at the school. I just shook my head with a smile of amazement as I thought about the student and kept walking.

It is these types of beliefs that cause hysteria among certain boards of education when it comes to the decision of placing police officers in schools and starting an SRO pro-gram. As I mentioned in the beginning of the book, I am employed in Meriden, CT, which is centrally located in the state. The bordering town to the northwest of Meriden is called Southington. (Please, you foreigners, pronounce it Suth-ing-ton not SOUTH-ing-ton.)

Southington Public High School also has a school resource officer. However, due to the paranoia of certain public officials, Officer Gerry Triano's role was the subject of intense debate. In his scenario, the Southington Board of Education encouraged Triano (their first SRO) to be uniformed and armed. Amazingly, it was the board of police commissioners that was against the idea of putting an armed officer in the school! They felt that the presence of an armed, uniformed officer would be a "distraction to the learning environment." Here is an example of a board of education thinking like police officers, and police representatives thinking like educators. But these are the types of debates that arise when a new program is being implemented. Everyone's an expert and thinks that they have the right answer when, in actuality, the SRO is the one who has to live with the decisions and should have the most input.

In the case of the Southington Police Department, it was decided that Officer Triano would have discretion on whether to go to the high school armed in uniform or in plain clothes. After about a year of sometimes wearing the uniform and gun (and sometimes not), Officer Triano made the decision that it would be best if he did wear his uniform and pistol at all times when at the school. As of 2002, he started his seventh year as Southington High's SRO and was still armed and uniformed. (Triano left the SRO position a short time later.)

The Board of Education and the Board of Police Commissioners agreed to grant Triano's request regarding his gun and uniform after listening to his reasons. What were these reasons? The same as any SRO would give in order to be armed in a public building, let alone a building housing 2,200 students as Southington High did. An officer automatically has a higher appearance of authority when he is in full uniform. Some people might not get the point when talking to a man dressed in a shirt and tie. But when someone's talking to a police officer in full uniform, they know they're having a conversation with an important person.

Another reason an SRO should demand to carry a gun is so that he can assist his fellow officers and help on crimes that occur near the school. I can't tell you how many times I've been in the school when I've heard over my police radio that a nearby officer is in need of assistance and I know that I'm the closest available unit. I don't want to imagine responding to a serious call near the school without a gun. In fact, there is a bank about an eighth of a mile from Platt High School. Should it ever be robbed, I would probably be the first responding unit. How could anyone allow an officer to be unarmed in such a situation?

The most obvious reason an SRO should carry a gun is to deter any students from bringing—and possibly using—one in school. An armed police officer would be a giant obstacle for a would-be shooter to encounter. Just an armed SRO's presence alone would make the student reconsider.

I can honestly say that I would never have accepted the position of school resource officer if the criteria included an unarmed presence. In my opinion, such an endeavor would be ludicrous. How can a municipality in its right mind put an unarmed law enforcement officer inside a public school—a mini-city? In light of the numerous school shootings throughout the country, several of which involved security guards or SROs, how can anyone justify putting an unarmed officer in a school—or for that matter, any setting? If you are an aspiring school resource officer and hope to be assigned to a school, think long and hard if you are willing to accept the position if your department tells you that you'll be ON DUTY there without a gun. This is a serious consideration.

All this brings us back to the students and where they get their knowledge of firearms. Not surprisingly, most of the students learn everything they know about guns from television or film. Many students were amazed—even confused—when I talked to them about the reality of firing a gun. I started my discussion by referring to something they could all relate to—movies. I take a popular character or movie such as *Lethal Weapon* or *Die Hard*, and I explained to the classes that it's very easy to tell these films are fake and unrealistic. When they asked me how, I asked for a show of hands on how many students have ever fired a gun before. In an average class of 20 students, I usually got a show of two or three hands. They explained that their father took them hunting or they belonged to gun clubs, etc. I then told the rest of the class that those movies are all fake because they all have sequels. Still confused, the students asked me to elaborate. I continued, saying that if Bruce Willis or Mel Gibson really shot that many rounds from their original movies in real life, there would be no sequels because both men would be deaf from the amount of ammunition they shot without ear protection. Many people (not just students) are ignorant when it comes to the report of a gun. I described to the students that the sound is extremely loud and that officers in training are required to wear ear protection to protect their eardrums.

I then explained the difficulty of aiming and actually hitting what one shoots at. Again, most people believe that it's easy to hit a target. Just point and shoot, right? Those of us with experience in shooting know better. I demonstrated the modified-Weaver stance that I use whenever I shoot. I pointed to a piece of paper hanging on the back wall and explain that if I wanted to hit that paper with a bullet I could, but I would need to aim and concentrate, not just "point and shoot." Then I asked the class to visualize a criminal running at me with a knife having the sole intention to kill me. I asked the class if they thought that might affect my poise or concentration and they almost all nodded in the affirmative. It's a very effective demonstration.

I stressed to the class that they absolutely cannot rely on TV and movies to give them an accurate depiction of gun usage. I give them the example of the ending in *Die Hard with a Vengeance* (can you tell I'm a movie buff?) where Bruce Willis's character, Lt. John McClane, shoots at a high voltage electrical wire that is fifty feet away, at night, while he is being shot at from a helicopter. He hits the wire, causing it to break and tangle with the helicopter's rotary blades, subsequently ending the film. I stressed to the class that if anyone had that type of shooting skill he would probably be kept under observation and study by the government. Or he would possibly be a frequent gold medalist in the biathlon event in the Winter Olympics.

In any event, I had wanted to create an atmosphere at the school where I could talk to the students on a group level. Thanks to several interested teachers, I was given that opportunity and thereby put my foot in the door, so to speak, in conducting class presentations at the school.

*   *   *

Speaking in classes and giving presentations was just one of the things I did to pass time when I first started as a school resource officer. Slowly but surely I would become aware of other issues which needed to be addressed. One such issue was the pedestrian traffic on the surrounding streets when school was dismissed. It was abominable. In fact, even before I became an SRO, I (and other officers) would be sent to the streets adjacent to the schools to monitor the students walking home because they would constantly walk in the roadway. Now that Platt High School and nearby Lincoln Middle School both had school resource officers, it was no longer the patrol division's responsibility, but mine and Officer Kristin Muir's (Lincoln's SRO). And did we have our hands full.

I'll never forget that first day driving down South Vine St. This street had the busiest pedestrian traffic in the area because students from the high school and middle school used it at just about the same time. If you drove down this street at 2:15 p.m. you would have thought that a concert let out.

On that first day there were more students in the road than on the sidewalk. Kristin and I knew we had to do something because we were going to be here everyday and we could not just turn our heads as these kids illegally walked in the middle of the road. It would only be a matter of time before somebody was going to get hit by a car. Besides, the students were causing a traffic nightmare. There were enough cars waiting to pick up students as it was. We didn't need the pedestrians in the road slowing down the vehicles, too. We needed to get those cars out of there as quickly as possible.

During those first few months of our SRO experience, Kristin and I would meet at a nearby parking lot that was close to both schools. Remember, the Board of Education refused to give us offices so we had to sit in our cars when things were quiet. Kristin and I would discuss our respective schools and how we could help each other out; but we also talked about the South Vine Street fiasco. What were we going to do? How were we going to enforce the sidewalk rule? Enter "Operation: Sidewalk."

After several days of planning, we decided that for the first week we would put our police cruisers' public address system to use. Before my days as an SRO, I probably used my P.A. five times. It's not something I enjoyed doing. Your voice is thrown outside at an incredible volume and everyone is turning to stare at who's talking. It was very similar to starting conversations with strange students. I was not the type of person who liked bringing attention to myself.

Today I am in love with the P.A.

I used it almost everyday during the school year. That first week, Kristin and I were all over those kids. We'd give them warnings and tell them that starting next week we would be issuing tickets to everyone that was walking in the road. It worked like a charm. Within one week, I'd have to estimate that 80% of the kids walking home were on the sidewalk. Of course you're always going to get those students that test you. But that's okay; we were prepared.

The following week, we issued about four tickets to students walking in the road. In Connecticut, a person must be over 16 to be issued an infraction. If we encountered any juveniles in the road, we either gave them a warning, brought them to their parents, or brought them to the police station. Kristin and I often selected the middle option.

It is quite amazing how a ticket issued to a high school teenager will single-handedly change the behavior of an entire school. Now, I've warned students on a variety of rule violations: everything from smoking in the bathroom to walking in the hall without a pass. I've come to the conclusion that a warning doesn't even come close to having the same effect as a ticket—where one must pay a fine.

The above figure of an 80% sidewalk compliance rate shot up to about 99% when the kids realized that we were either issuing them tickets or bringing them home to mommy. It was almost miraculous. Within one month, Kristin and I had transformed a street from looking like the Boston Marathon into a legally conforming, driving-conducive thoroughfare. Just like any aspect of society, there will always be those who disobey the rules. Kristin and I continued to issue pedestrian violation tickets and gave juvenile offenders a ride home to their parent(s). But the transformation of what the street once was to what it became is a prime example of what can happen when you team up with another officer to try and solve a problem.

Kristin and I partnered up on many other situations. Whenever we got word that a fight was going to break out at a specific location, one of us would wait at that spot while the other would follow the involved students just to make sure no violence occurred.

Platt High and Lincoln Middle School are also near some wooded areas. The two of us learned real fast that students liked to smoke marijuana in the woods. Quite a few times we would sneak up on the unsuspecting students and catch them in the act. This led to several arrests and, on one occasion, I found a knife on a student. This occurred in the morning before school started which means the student was probably going to bring the knife into the building. Not a good thing. He ended up getting expelled.

The examples listed above are not described in order to give Officer Muir and me a pat on the back. Rather, they demonstrate and prove the effectiveness of teamwork and cooperation with another SRO. Even if you're not as lucky as I was to have another school resource officer 100 yards from you, there are always other options. Officer Mike Lane, the SRO at Washington Middle School on the other side of the city, would frequently have the traffic officer assist him during dismissal to curb the fighting problem he had with students after school. Teaming up with another officer is beneficial for all involved. It helps the SRO because it gives him another tool to use in the performance of his school related duties. It helps the other officer because it gives him the opportunity to see

SCHOOL RESOURCE OFFICER: FUNCTIONING AS A COP IN TODAY'S HIGH SCHOOL

the SRO's duties and it introduces him to the students of the school. Do what you can to incorporate other officers into your enforcement. <u>Students become nonchalant when they see the same officer every day at their school. They lose sight that their SRO is still a member of the police department and has many tools at his disposal.</u> When the students see you teaming up with other officers it opens their eyes to the fact that you really are a real cop.

*   *   *

Before I continue describing my typical daily routine at the school, allow me to throw in what some of you might consider a surprising statement:

I was miserable during my first year as a school resource officer.

Yes, you read that correctly. MISERABLE. "Why then," I hear you asking yourself, "did he write a book on the subject?" Because things progressively got better, and I want to make sure that you don't commit to a position that you may not enjoy.

During my first year as an SRO I thought of leaving the school and returning to my usual duties as a patrol officer. However, like most of you, I am not one to give up that easily. I almost did, though. <u>For starters, the job was boring.</u> The school administrators were not exactly sure how to utilize me and I in turn was not sure of what they expected of me. The same can be said for some of the other SROs, too. For the longest time, Kristin would be a taxi service for the middle school students. The administrators would ask her to bring kids home that had just been suspended or that wore clothing that was inappropriate. It was almost embarrassing.

68

Here is an officer who was once involved in a deadly force incident, now being relegated to bring Molly home because her skirt is too short. But Kristin didn't give up either.

Besides the boredom, I was shocked at the attitude of the students. As I mentioned earlier, many students simply had no concept of what respect was. That is probably what unnerved me the most. The swearing, the sexual innuendoes, the disrespect toward teachers, the clothing, and the immaturity were all factors that stemmed from a lack of respect—both inward and toward others. Be prepared is all I can say. Again, my intention is not to dissuade anyone from becoming an SRO. I simply want those who are thinking about taking the position to be wary of all the aspects. Just as there are plenty of reasons why I wanted to leave the school, there are also plenty on why I chose to stay. I stayed, after all, three more years, didn't I?

But since I am still describing my initial months at the school, I feel I should also describe the emotions I felt at that time. And my emotions at the time were shock and dismay. I had no idea how chaotic a public school could be; but I was the one who quickly realized that I needed to adapt to the situation because it wasn't going to adapt to me. When I first joined the school, I learned that, although the teachers weren't impressed with all the students, they were also not as dejected as I was. Seeing this led me to believe that I needed to give my new position a chance so that I could get used to the environment.

Since I've mentioned teachers, I must confess that they were also a reason why I was not happy those first few months. Not because of anything they did. (You'll soon read how I have nothing but the utmost respect for our educators.) No, the teachers—and the entire faculty for that matter—contributed to my angst because I didn't know any of them! I was a total stranger in a strange land. I went from knowing everyone at the police station (from the mechanic to the chief), to not knowing a single person at the school. This was very intimidating to say the least, and combined with all the other difficulties I was having in the beginning of that first year, it made me question if I had made the right decision.

But then something amazing happened. The school utilized me. And not just a little bit. Day by day, the people in the school (administrators, teachers, and students) started to request my services. And once the snowball started to roll, it grew bigger and bigger. I started to feel needed and liked. It was a wonderful feeling.

Students from the school newspaper interviewed me so that they could write an article about me. Teachers asked me if they could bring their classes on field trips to the police station with me as the tour guide. I was asked to pose for the yearbook photo since I was now considered part of the faculty. Mr. Tom Smith, an English teacher, asked if I would read a story, *Killing Mr. Griffin*, and talk about it in his class and comment on the law enforcement aspect of the book. Mr. Peter Trosell, a math teacher, asked me to talk to his class on how math relates to police work. I actually lucked out on that one since I had taken two advanced classes on accident investigation. I got up and showed the class how speed can be derived from basic skid marks using the formula $s=v(30*d*f)$. But I digress...

The police department, too, began giving more support to the program. Lt. Thorp, my supervisor at the time, began holding weekly meetings with the four SROs to track our progress and address any concerns we may have had. Thorp, probably more than anyone else, wanted the project to succeed. After all, it was his baby. He was the one mostly responsible for bringing the school resource officer program to the police department. He made it a priority to be the liaison between the Meriden Police Department and the Board of Education.

The department also began sending the SROs to more training classes and conferences than we had ever gone to before. In the past, when I was still on patrol, it was difficult to get sent to any type of training class because the department would have to hire another officer to replace me during my shift. This meant paying the hired officer overtime. Needless to say, the brass wasn't enthusiastic about doing that too often.

Now that I was an SRO, the department didn't have to hire anyone to replace me when I wasn't in the school. If I was not there on a given day, the school would just have to make do without me. Again, I was lucky to have Kristin right across the street. We would cover for each other countless times. If she was ever out sick, her school knew that they could call me and I would go right over. The same thing happened if I ever missed a day. Platt High would call over to Lincoln Middle and ask them to send Kristin over. This type of cooperation helped each of us to become familiar with one another's students.

Since the department didn't have to worry about paying to replace the SROs when they were out, we began to notice an increase in our training sessions. The four of us would get sent (as a group or separately) to many classes related to school violence or juvenile matters. Some of the classes, such as Danny Holland's "Kids & Khemicals," are excellent and highly recommended.

Holland has experience as a school resource officer and is the president of Parent & Teen Universities, Inc., which is described on their web site as, "a concept geared toward helping parents better connect with their teenage children." For more information on Parent & Teen Universities, Inc., visit them on the World Wide Web at www.p-t-u.org.

With everything starting to fall into place, I began to get very busy at the school. And I was beginning to realize what a great bunch of people the staff was. I'll discuss teachers in more detail later on, but suffice it to say that most people have no idea what an amazing and dedicated group of instructors they have in their public schools.

In addition to all these positive experiences, I was also asked to attend as many of the school's sporting events as possible. This proposition ended up being beneficial for both the school and me. The school ended up gaining an extra officer for their sporting events that made the administrators happy, especially since I already knew most of the students in attendance. I profited from the deal because, although I would not get paid for my time at the football or basketball games, I would earn compensatory time, which I could accumulate and use at a later date. For example, if I earned four hours for working a football game, I could put that four hours in my compensatory time account and take four hours off at a later time. The Meriden Police Department allowed the SROs to amass up to 24 hours of comp time. By the time Christmas vacation rolled around, I would combine my 3 days off (24 hrs. ÷ 8 hr. work days = 3 days) with my regular vacation time and get the same amount of days off as the students. I worked so many sporting events that I ended up taking off every day the students had off—except summer vacation, of course. This was an extremely big perk of the position, as I was able to take much more time off than I would ever have been able to as a patrolman.

I was now no longer bored as a school resource officer, and I wouldn't be bored again. Those early days of always wondering if anything would happen quickly disappeared. I routinely stayed at the police department finishing cases well after my quitting time of 3:00 p.m. (I tried to leave the school at about 2:45 p.m.)

My days were filled with agendas: student mediations, classroom presentations, traffic duties, meetings with parents, meetings with my supervisors, investigations into illegal activities, arrests, parking violations, truancy issues, trespassers, assisting other officers, dealing with student informants, coordinating special events, and fights. Those are just a sampling of what a typical day can consist of in a normal school year. Some of these issues I've already covered; more will be discussed in the next chapter. For now, I want to shift gears temporarily and talk about another facet of the SRO position that you may not have foreseen, but nevertheless exists. It's about a group of people that you will have to deal with who constantly give you grief about your position: your brother officers.

* * *

I felt that I needed to include this brief but important topic in the middle of describing my duties as an SRO since many fellow officers believe the position is simple. So let me just warn you now. Be prepared for the jokes.

SCHOOL RESOURCE OFFICER: FUNCTIONING AS A COP IN TODAY'S HIGH SCHOOL

As if you didn't have enough to contend with at your assigned school, get ready for your comrades-in-arms to have quite a few laughs at your expense. If you take an SRO position, you will forever become known as the "school cop." Such descriptors will be coupled with the unavoidable SRO quips. "Did you arrest anyone for cutting in the lunch line today," I would hear. Or, "What'd this kid do...forget to cover his books?"

Here, again, is where your personality comes into play. Most of the barbs I heard were actually pretty funny and I would laugh at them. But I wouldn't let it stop there. I'd have to give back my own jab so that the officer wouldn't feel left out. The jokes about my position never bothered me and, when I think about it, I'd probably make the same jokes if the roles were reversed. The other three SROs were victims of the same ribbing, and they too just laughed it off. We understood since we were in a relatively new position and weren't seen by our peers for most of the day that many officers believed we didn't do anything and had a "cake" job. Many were also jealous of the schedule of the SRO position. Working Monday through Friday from 7:00 a.m. to 3:00 p.m. is not a bad gig. Then again, as you recall, there were only six volunteers for the position when it was announced.

The point I'm trying to make is that here is an instance when your flexible personality comes into play yet again. I know several officers within my department that are more than willing to dish out the insults and jokes, but when they become the subjects of laughter they get upset and angry. Instead of continuing the back and forth bantering and having a good time with it, they shut down and give the silent treatment. Such a personality would never survive in an

74

SRO position, not just because of the officers' jokes but also because of the students'!

Some police officers get very defensive when they are teased by their peers regarding a specialized position to which they have been assigned. How you handle the situation will be determined by your attitude and social characteristics. Just be advised that you will hear the comments and wisecracks from the "real cops." But keep in mind that the partnership you're building with the youth of your community will pay off much more than if you were still working regular patrol. Everyday detectives and patrolmen try to make contacts throughout the city to aid their investigations. Every year, at Platt High School, I gained 250 new contacts. These contacts were part of the incoming freshman class that I would be with for the next four years. In my four years at the school, I got to know quite a lot of people who walked the halls of Platt High and still reside in Meriden. This has given me an enormous advantage when I have had to deal with those former students in a criminal investigation. My knowledge of many former students and their interactions with me has helped me immensely when I'm on the street dealing with them.

So let your buddies on the force make fun. With the amount of contacts an SRO can establish, it will be the school resource officer who has the last laugh.

SCHOOL CRIMES

I've already covered several of my duties on a typical day at the high school. You've read about my classroom presentations and my occasional assistance to nearby officers. I've described my relationships with confidential student informants, and how Officer Kristin Muir and I teamed up to control the pedestrian violations on a nearby street.

But what about the rest? What are the other duties? Are you wondering what my most common task at the school was? Or the most common criminal problem at the school? Was it fighting? Drugs?

From my conversations with the many school resource officers that I know, I've gathered that each school's administrators utilize their SROs in their own unique way. Officer Sal Nesci, for example, made traffic duties during school arrival and dismissal a priority, where for me it was not a big deal if I happened to miss dismissal traffic because my school was located at a much less busy throughway.

One of Officer Mike Lane's biggest priorities at Washington Middle School was to follow the large groups of students that walked home after dismissal. Frequently these students would start fighting when they got far enough away from the school. Officer Lane's presence helped cut down the violence dramatically.

My most common function at the school was assisting the two vice principals, Mr. Shugrue and Mr. Paluszewski, with student mediations. A student mediation involves an assistant principal and/or a school resource officer, plus at least two students who want to kick the living crap out of each other. It was a rare day when I was not sitting in on at least one mediation. Some days we had five. And the frustrating thing about them is that they were all the same. "Francis" hears from a "good source" that "Leon" is "talking junk" about him. Francis then confronts Leon in a not-so-calm way and the two exchange heated words, resulting in a situation that almost leads to fisticuffs. The next thing you know, Francis and Leon are both in the main office conference room with me and an assistant principal. Each student is allowed to speak freely without the other's interruption and in most instances the mediation concludes with both students realizing that the "good source" from which they heard the rumor was not so good after all. The two students realize that their argument was baseless and agree that there will be no further problem.

That is an example of what Mr. Shugrue and I have termed "he said/she said" arguments. They were by far the most common types of mediations. Students are either extremely gullible or very touchy. Either way, they do not take lightly to the fact that another student may have been talking about him/her. They take serious umbrage knowing that they may have been "dissed" or "played." A majority of these mediations end up revealing that nothing even close to the accusation was ever made. Nevertheless, students will always be defending themselves regardless if they heard it from the student in question or some other "reliable" source.

Another type of mediation that I encountered at Platt High School was almost identical to the "he said/she said." In fact, it can still be labeled with that name. However the only difference is that this mediation was purposely caused by a small group of students that the principals and I called the Don Kings. Not to be confused with the Latin Kings, the Don Kings are a select number of students who intentionally start rumors between students that they would like to see engage in a fight. Just like their namesake, these students are nothing more than fight promoters who come to school in hopes of seeing a melee. It's their favorite form of entertainment.

When a Don King started a malicious rumor between two students, it was almost guaranteed that those two students would end up in a mediation with me. This type of fight promoting is very costly to the school system as it pulled the administrators and me from other issues that we could have been dealing with. Although we knew who the Don Kings were, it was difficult to prove that they were the catalyst for the arguments and fights.

Every school has their share of Don Kings. As an SRO, it is your duty to quickly find out who they are and make sure that they know that you're aware of their practices and that you won't be taking them lightly.

The Don Kings' instigations led to some of the most violent fights at the school. I recall one fight from the 2001/2002 school year where one freshman student walked into the boys bathroom and sucker-punched another student. As if the blow wasn't bad enough, when the victim fell down his head struck a steel beam, which led to a very bloody head wound. Although the victim was all right, his assault was the consequence of some Don King students egging on the aggressor and telling him that the victim had been disrespecting him.

As a result of that attack, the aggressor was arrested and sent to juvenile court. I was unable to prove the Don Kings' role in the attack, but the administration and I were well aware of their involvement. The only way that I could curtail a Don King's provoking behavior was to speak with him on a frequent basis so that he knew I was aware of his actions. I would also strictly enforce any rules that they broke so that they understood that I could be tough when needed, although I would always tell them that if they stopped "promoting" fights in the school that I would loosen up on my rigid adherence to school policy and treat them like normal students. I found that this would work for several weeks but then the Dons would fall back to their entertainment through promotion. The Don Kings were a problem that required constant attention in order to limit the amount of damage they did.

*   *   *

The "he said/she said" rumors and the Don Kings often led to a physical confrontation. Platt High School has a zero-tolerance policy for fighting. Any students found to be fighting or engaging in violent behavior would be arrested and suspended for ten days. Obviously, self-defense is allowed, but only if used necessarily and reasonably.

There has been much discussion about the impact of zero-tolerance and whether it is effective. Most of the school resource officer conferences I've attended preach that zero-tolerance is not as useful as once thought. The tragedies at Columbine and Paducah (as well as others) have scared and forced school systems to come up with a "quick fix" method of curbing all types of violence. The solution includes zero-tolerance, which I believe contains good arguments for and against its implementation. On the one hand, using zero-tolerance in a school means that everyone will be treated the same. Students will not be able to complain that they are not dealt with fairly or that one fight should have involved police action while another should not. On the other hand, zero-tolerance leads to enforcement of superfluous violations. Whereas in the 1960's and 1970's school yard fights were almost expected with the "boys will be boys" rationale, today even the slightest physical contact between students can lead to a court appearance.

Your particular school administration will decide whether to conform to zero-tolerance policies. This does not mean that the SRO must make an arrest for every single violent incident. After all, the officer still needs probable cause. When a fight broke out in the school, the administration conducted their own investigation while I performed my own. I can recall only one time when the administrators and I did not agree on an outcome. The school felt that a fight did indeed occur and suspended the students involved. I could not come up with enough evidence to pursue the matter, yet I felt in my heart that a disturbance did occur. Out of dozens of fighting incidents, this was the only variance between the administrators and me.

It is difficult to measure whether the zero-tolerance fighting policy at Platt High School has resulted in an increased, decreased, or unchanged amount of fighting. Prior to my assignment to the school, Platt High would only contact the police for the most serious of matters. Now, they are able to prosecute many more incidents since an SRO is stationed at the school. Not surprisingly, this indicated a major rise in crimes reported and prosecuted since I was assigned to the school. However, has an officer's presence made a difference in the amount of violent behavior exhibited?

The principal and most teachers say it has. Many of the faculty members used to come up to me and say that there were nowhere near as many fights as compared to before an SRO was at the school. However, a small percentage of teachers also said that there was no difference. Unfortunately, there is no way to know for sure because most of the fights that occurred prior to my arrival at the school went unreported to the police. I am grateful, however, that almost every single faculty member had approached me and told me that my presence at the school had made for a much improved overall school environment.

Oddly enough, the majority of fights have occurred on either a Tuesday or Thursday. And the most common time was usually right after the lunch wave concluded at 12:15 p.m. The time does not surprise me since that was when all the students—who have been making fun of each other for the last half hour in the lunch hallway—exited the cafeteria area and converged with the rest of the students. What does surprise me is the fact that Tuesday and Thursday had the most incidents of fighting. I have no explanation for this at all. Perhaps the analysis of why Platt High School students were more apt to fight on those days is best left for a psychiatrist. I can, however, vouch for the full-moon theory. It is not a superstition. Having worked as a police officer for four years in a diverse, public high school, I can say with conviction that a full moon does affect a student's behavior. How does it affect them? Let's just say that if you have any vacation time you should use them on days that have full moons.

A full moon affects a student's behavior just as much as a rainy day. I lived for rainy school days. They were the most quiet and peaceful days of the school year, matched only by snowy days. Again, this is something I cannot prove but my experience has shown me that precipitation affects students' behavior and subliminally compels them to be calm.

On the other hand, if you're experiencing a beautiful day with the temperature in the high seventies or low eighties, you're almost in full-moon territory. Come into school ready to go because the weather is comfortable which means the students will be active. Obviously I have no proof of why the above-cited incidents occur when they do. All I have are m statistics and my experience, which have shown the above to be true. But don't take my word for it. Any one of Platt's teachers will tell you the same thing.

Before I continue with the discussion on fighting, it's time for me to give you another tool of the trade. You may be wondering how I discovered the days and times that fighting is most prevalent. There is a very good computer program called *School COP* available for school resource officers. It is available for download at www.schoolcopsoftware.com. Best of all, it's free! I had this program installed on one of the computers in the library of the

82

school since I didn't have an office at the time. (Did I mention that already?) *School Cop* tracks all the incidents that take place in your school. It even lets you scan a plan of your school into the program so that you can plot points and keep track of where events take place. For example, not only will the program tell you when most of your fights occur, but it will also plot onto the school map where each and every fight took place. It will also track all types of incidents, not just fights. I highly recommend this software to all SROs. It has accurately helped me track the incidents in my school so that I was able take corrective action. The only drawback to this program is that it is not available for the Macintosh operating system, which is my favorite platform.

Other law enforcement-specific software—including another SRO program—are available for Palm PDA's (personal digital assistants). You can check out all the applications at

http://www.cybercop-software.com/lesoftware.htm.

Such programs have aided me in graphing crimes and pinpointing their frequent locations. I became much more mentally prepared on Tuesdays and Thursdays since discovering that those two days produced the most fights. This does not mean that I was taken by surprise when a fight broke out on any other day. An SRO must always be careful when dealing with students who are out of control and acting violently. Whenever a fight occurred while I was at the school, I would usually get paged over the school radio to respond to the area in question. The brawl was usually over by the time I arrived as nearby teachers had separated the combatants. On a few occasions I would be the first to respond and break up the raucous, but this was rare since the fight usually took place away from my location.

Students will first take problems out of SRO's sight.

I don't mean to give the impression that Platt High School was filled with donnybrooks for a majority of the school year. On the contrary, Platt averaged about one fight per month, which in my estimation, is a pretty good percentage when you take into consideration that 1,000 students are cohabiting with each other everyday.

When the two (or more) students were finally separated, they would be brought to the main office and held in two separate rooms. The school administrators and I would then begin our own investigations. My first step was to talk to each student individually. The first thing I would look for when speaking with them is any type of injury or bruise to their body. Scratches, scrapes, and bruises were a good start to give me probable cause that a fight had occurred even though I had not witnessed it.

Next, I would interview the students involved. Just like when I worked in patrol, I would get two different stories. Seldom would I ever get the same story from both parties. However, another advantage of working with the students every day is that they learn to trust you and sometimes that will allow them to break down and tell you the truth. This does not happen for every student, but it happens much more than it would on street patrol because many of the students are your friends and know you can help them if they cooperate.

The most difficult aspect of investigating a fight between two students is differentiating between a mutual fight and self-defense. I told students that they were allowed to defend themselves from any injury. I explained to them that they should do whatever is necessary to escape harm; this includes running away, putting desks or people in between themselves and the aggressor, or even hitting back if the aggressor will not let up. However, I made it clear to the students that there is a definite distinction between self-defense and an assault. If the aggressor is no longer a threat and the other student begins beating on him to the point where now the aggressor is the helpless victim, the tables have just turned and a mutual fight has developed.

Another key element to discovering what exactly happened during an altercation is to interview as many witnesses as possible. Very rarely did a fight occur when no one was around. The student population itself (over 1,000 kids) made it difficult for a fight to go unnoticed. Usually there were at least a couple of teachers who witnessed the scuffle, as well as several nearby students. While teachers and faculty members always gave me information pertaining to the fight, students were not always so accommodating. This is yet another instance of where good rapport with your student body comes into play.

When I arrived to an area in the school where a fight had just taken place, I made a quick mental note of what students were in the area and thus probably witnessed the melee. I learned quickly that it was futile to ask students what they witnessed while they were standing in front of other students. No student in his right mind is going to step forward in front of his peers to "snitch" on the fighters.

Instead of asking them at the scene, I asked any teachers to describe what they saw. When I was finished, I went downstairs to the main office and sent for two or three of the students that were hanging around the fight area. I called them down one at a time so that no one else knew that they were talking to me. I then brought them into a private room and asked them what happened. Now that the student was alone and knew that his information was confidential, he felt much more comfortable and willing to tell me what had happened. Although this made the investigation a bit lengthier, it allowed for a more thorough and precise conclusion.

*   *   *

Fighting is just one of the criminal activities that takes place in a high school. Another issue—which I feel is the most damaging—is drug use. I am not aware of any high school that does not have students who use some type of illegal drug. And although this is not a book to list statistics and facts about high school drug use (there are plenty books on the subject), I will say that www.whitehousedrugpolicy.gov has excellent updated numbers that detail the juvenile drug problem in America.

As you may or may not know, marijuana (as of this writing) is the number one drug of choice among high school students. The preceding federal Web site confirms that fact. My own experience supports that fact because marijuana was the only drug I have ever found on students' possession at the school. Marijuana's easy accessibility and relatively cheap price makes it popular among high school students. Here again, the school had taken a zero-tolerance stance, which I firmly supported. I have always believed that drugs lead to other major problems down the road—in fact, many studies support this idea—and they do nothing but contribute to the decline of society. This is one of the reasons that I wholeheartedly supported the Board of Education's policy of expelling a student who has been found with drugs on his person.

hearsay

The majority of my drug arrests in the school stemmed from tips given to me by my CSIs (Confidential Student Informants). The CSI would come to me during the school day, usually when classes were in session so that no one would see him with me, and tell me that he saw a certain student showing off some marijuana or trying to sell it to another student.

As you can probably foresee, dealing with the issue of drug possession leads us into the subject of searching students and their belongings. This is a very tricky area and admittedly, at times, confusing. Depending on what state you're working in, laws for search and seizure can differ. Although the following discussion will deal mostly with federal law and how it pertains to SROs and school administrators in general, it will still be beneficial to SROs around the country who work in their respective states. Nevertheless, it is important for you to be very familiar with your state's search and seizure regulations.

The following is a paragraph taken right out of Platt High School's student handbook:

> Lockers and desks are the property of the school and shall be subject to inspection by an authorized administrator. Students shall not bring to school or keep on their persons or in the lockers or desks any objects or materials which are dangerous to the health or safety of themselves or others. Included in this category of prohibited objects and materials are illegal drugs.
>
> No student shall keep or store in a locker assigned to him/her for his/her use any item the possession of which is illegal or in violation of school regulations or which endangers the health, safety or welfare of self or others (such as matches, chemicals, ammunition, weapons, drugs, alcoholic beverages, etc.)

Most students don't bother to read their handbook. I know I didn't when I went to high school. The reason I know that they don't read it is because whenever I made my classroom presentations, they'd ask me questions that were clearly answered in the handbook. One of the most frequent questions dealt with the topic of searching students and the rights that they have. I found that many of the students were extremely ignorant when it came to their rights and what a teacher or principal can do to them. For example, many students believe that teachers cannot lay a finger on them. This is just not so. Although it sometimes does appear that that may be the case, especially since many teachers themselves think they cannot touch students, most states' laws clearly authorize school personnel to do what is necessary to control a student who is being disruptive and dangerous to the school welfare. As a matter of fact, my ignorance came to light on a recent seminar in New Orleans where I got a chance to meet with dozens of SROs and administrators from around the country. I almost fell over in disbelief when an Alabama superintendent told me that her state still practices corporal punishment. Although most states in America do not still practice that type of discipline, they do allow school officials to use physical force on students when necessary. In Connecticut, teachers may use physical force on students "to (1) protect himself or others from immediate physical injury, (2) to obtain possession of a dangerous instrument or controlled substance, (3) to protect property from physical damage, or (4) to restrain a minor student or to remove a minor student to another area to maintain order." (*A Practical Guide to Connecticut School Law*, p. 187)

Surprisingly, many teachers and administrators are scared to use force on students even when it is necessary to do so. Due to the overwhelming amount of frivolous lawsuits pending in our country's courts, educators feel that they could lose their job and incur punitive damages if they lay a finger on a student. I believe it is an SRO's responsibility to make sure teachers know their rights and that they most definitely are allowed to use reasonable force on a student if one of the above-mentioned criteria is met.

Turning back to the subject of students and their rights during a search, there is a whole span of different beliefs that the students have. Some think that nothing of theirs can be searched; some believe that only some areas, such as lockers and desks, can be searched; still other students feel that everything is open to a search. And then there's the issue of who can actually do the searching. We've already read the Board of Education's policy on searching. Now let's take a look at what the Constitution says about a police search. Hopefully, for most of you this will only be a review.

The Fourth Amendment of the United States Constitution states that "no warrants shall issue, but upon probable cause, supported by oath or affirmation, and particularly describing the place to be searched, and the persons or things to be seized." Clearly, the key phrase in that statement is "probable cause." Herein lies the difference between the police and school administrators. It is much easier for administrators to justify a search than it is for a police officer. According to the United States Supreme Court, school authorities only need reasonable suspicion of a crime to conduct a search whereas police officers need probable cause. Probable cause (for those who don't know) is

89

defined as "facts and circumstances that would lead a reasonable person to believe that a crime has been committed."

Unless they are experts in case law, most police officers only know a handful of Supreme Court cases that are relevant to their profession. A couple that come to mind are *Terry v. Ohio* and *Miranda v. Arizona*.

Let me add a new court case to the memory banks of every SRO out there. Take a moment and thank your lucky stars for the ruling on *New Jersey v. T.L.O.* In my opinion, this is the landmark case for school administrators and school resource officers. Why, you ask? I'll try to be brief.

T.L.O. was significant because if gave students rights under the fourth amendment. The Court ruled that students could not be searched on a whim and without reason. The Court further ruled that school administrators are agents of the government and needed to abide by the fourth amendment. HOWEVER (it's a big however) the Court made two crucial modifications for school administrators. It stated that school officials would not have to obtain warrants to conduct searches due to the impracticality of this requirement in a school setting and "the need to assure a safe school environment." (*A Practical Guide to Connecticut School Law*, p. 205)

The Court also ruled that school officials need only reasonable suspicion to conduct a search on students rather than the more stringent probable cause that police need. This ruling of using reasonable suspicion seemed to be a compromise between giving students full fourth amendment rights and letting school officials continue their role as a replacement to parents during the day.

Knowing that the administrators in my school needed less criteria than I did to perform a search was frustrating, but it was better than having them meet my standards, too. This way, at least, the school authorities can take steps to protect the rest of the school population when they feel that one or more students pose a threat to everyone else.

Whenever one of my confidential student informants approached me with information on a student carrying drugs, I would bring that informant to an assistant principal so that the administrator could get the information. This way, the administrator could make the decision to search simply based on the informant's statement. In some cases where I believed that I may have had probable cause to make the search, I still had the student report to the administrator since his criteria for a search was lower than mine. This is how a majority of SROs told me that they handled their searches as well. Remember, thanks to *T.L.O.*, it is usually better and safer for the school to work with the lower requirement (reasonable suspicion) rather than the higher, more difficult requirement (probable cause).

But how far can a search go?

As I mentioned earlier, I had the opportunity to go to New Orleans, Louisiana, for a three-day, national seminar on SROs titled "COPS in Schools: Keeping Our Kids Safe." (All the police stayed in a hotel smack-dab in the middle of Bourbon St. I'll save the nightlife stories for another time). During the first day of training, I had the pleasure of listening to Dr. Bernard James of Pepperdine University's School of Law. James has an extensive background in school law and was able to clarify many questions that the SROs in attendance (including me) had.

The following examples come from the article "Legal Issues: School Safety and the Law," which was presented by Dr. James.

91

Now I always knew that there was a fine line between the actions an SRO took and those of a school administrator. For example, a legal case cited in the article presented the scenario of an SRO who was present at the search of a student by a school official. The official performed the search and requested the SRO's presence. Would this be a legal search or did the presence of the officer complicate matters and violate the student's fourth amendment rights? SROs rejoice! The appellate court ruled that the search was valid and reasonable under the *New Jersey v. T.L.O.* standard. The court ruled that since the educator initiated the search, he was held to the "reasonable suspicion" standard and the SRO did not affect that standard in any way.

So to all my new SROs out there...do not freak if you walk into a search conducted by an administrator. It's okay. But wait...there's even better news ahead.

Say little Johnny approaches the assistant principal and says that Kevin might have a knife on him. Now what if the administrator approaches the SRO and, because of the possibility of a weapon being involved, asks the SRO to search the student? What now? There is no probable cause for the officer to make the search. But there's plenty of reasonable suspicion for the school official to do so. Yet now the SRO is being asked to perform the search. Time to thank the Wisconsin Supreme Court for their ruling on *State of Wisconsin v. Angelia D.B.*

They ruled that the incident started as a school-based problem, not a law enforcement one. The school officials therefore had every right in this instance to use all tools within their grasp, including their school resource officer who is much more experienced in performing pat downs than the assistant principal. Because the investigation began and stayed school-oriented until the knife was found, the court ruled that the SRO has a right to search when asked by the administrator, especially when a weapon is involved. After the knife was found, the police took over the matter since a criminal law was broken.

Last example. In *In re: D.E.M. v. Commonwealth of Pennsylvania*, police told school officials of a middle school that they received a tip that student D.E.M. was carrying a gun on campus. Not having enough cause to follow up, the police left the school. However, the principal took the matter into his own hands and began his own investigation. He called D.E.M. to the office where he searched his person, bag, and later his jacket. The search turned up a knife on the student's person and a gun in the jacket. During D.E.M.'s trial, the court suppressed the evidence saying that the principal acted as an agent of the police and violated the student's fourth amendment rights. The appellate court reversed the ruling and stated that the principal searched the student to primarily ensure the safety of the rest of the student body. The court also stated that the police did not in any way coerce or direct the principal's actions, which fit under the *T.L.O.* reasonable suspicion ruling.

A significant point that Dr. James and the article raise is that the principal in the above example could also have used an SRO to perform the search just as in the previous example. In fact, because such serious weapons were involved, the principal should definitely have called for police support or at the very least assistance from additional school officials.

Looking back at the above examples from Dr. James, it's reasonable to conclude that the supreme courts of the land

93

understand the plight of school administrators in today's educational landscape while still trying to give students fourth amendment rights.

There is no doubt that the legal aspect of search and seizure in a school is an important matter. But if I ever found myself in a situation where I wasn't sure which way to approach a situation, or if I didn't know if I had the legal right to perform a search, I would have to act in a way that would be to the benefit of the safety of the school body. I firmly believe that the safety of the student body comes before the rights of any one particular student. And if you read the court rulings from the cases mentioned above, it seems that the justices seem to be leaning in that direction as well.

Now let me throw you another interesting question. What if the student that the principal wants to search, refuses to allow the search? Again, this will result in an answer that very well may differ from state to state. Connecticut has a statute which makes the interference of a search by a person authorized to do so (such as a school official) a crime. Theoretically, the student could be arrested if he refuses to be searched, since the school officials are allowed to perform the search as government agents, albeit with a couple of modifications to the Fourth Amendment.

My advice to those of you who are SROs is to not make school search and seizure more difficult than it is. You must remember that as a school resource officer you will be involved in two types of investigations: police initiated and school initiated. If you're involved in a police-initiated investigation, the same rules and laws must be followed as if you were on any other type of police investigation. Probable cause is needed for arrests and searches, and Miranda warnings must be given when the suspect is questioned in custody. For school-initiated investigations, the administrator makes the calls and uses the SRO as a tool for assistance, e.g. as a witness, to help search, etc. The school administrator needs only reasonable suspicion to conduct a search—although it is important to note that, like a police officer, the administrator's search cannot go beyond the scope of the item being sought. In other words, he cannot look in the student's change purse when he's looking for a gun.

One last note on search and seizure. The search of a student's person and effects (jacket, book bag, etc.) often lead to the oversight of another area that can be searched: the student's vehicle. (Again, here is where your own state law must be reviewed.) Many states, including Connecticut, consider the student's car to be property that can be searched if the *T.L.O.* reasonableness standard applies. Do not overlook this significant piece of property. If a student has been seen with a weapon but it cannot be found on him or anywhere in the building, there's a good chance that it is being kept inside the car. Don't forget, the car is parked on school property and considered an effect of the student available for search. Some school districts have gone so far as to include blanket consent-to-search forms which parents must sign if they want their children's cars allowed on the school property. I believe that these forms are very helpful in deterring students from bringing any type of contraband to the school.

The Fourth Amendment modifications that have been granted to school administrators by the Supreme Court are tools that should be used but not abused. In the ever changing school climate where gangs roam and guns are brought to classrooms, we (the SROs and school officials) need every break we can get in trying to curb the violence and drug abuse. SROs and school officials—when working together in a concerted effort—can use the *T.L.O.* case to keep their schools as safe and learning friendly as possible.

*   *   *

Knowing the boundaries between school policy and criminal law are essential for an SRO. As a police officer, I am very familiar with my state's penal code and the criminal statutes. When I entered the public high school as an SRO I was very confused as to what my power would be in regards to enforcing the school's code of conduct.

T.L.O. and the other aforementioned cases cleared all that up for me. As stated in some of the previously mentioned examples, the school administrators were free to use me as their agent. It was perfectly acceptable for them to ask me for my assistance in certain matters. This delegation extended to the enforcement of school policy. For example, one school rule listed in the code of conduct prohibits students from wearing coats in the building during classes. Initially, I did not enforce this rule because I felt there was no way I could deliver any consequences. I was used to handing out tickets or arresting people when they broke the law. But what was I to do to a student who disobeyed a school rule? Surely I couldn't arrest a student because he was wearing his coat. And did I have the authority to send students to the office if they didn't listen to me? (Rereading that sentence makes me laugh. Can you imagine not listening to a police officer and hearing him send you the office as a punishment? It's crazy but true.)

The answer to the last question is "yes." I was free to assist the educators in carrying out school policy. Remember my title: School **Resource** Officer. I was a resource to the school administrators in helping them carry out their duties of promoting a safe and stable school environment. Again, Dr. Bernard James puts it in perspective in his article:

> Under the direction of the educator, the SRO may, in effect, join the team of specialists that work together to achieve the education mission. These tasks may include enforcing the code of conduct and referring serious violators to the juvenile justice system.

"Enforcing the code of conduct" can have a whole range of definitions. In my school, I was only allowed to refer students to the assistant principals or escort them to the office. I am aware of other SROs who have been given the authority to issue after-school detentions to students that have violated a school rule. Such enforcement power is delegated by each separate school and board of education. Whatever school disciplinary powers given to the SRO, it is important to realize that the officer is acting as a resource to the educator and that he is not left to only enforcing criminal law.

∗   ∗   ∗

So we've talked about fighting. And we've talked about drugs and weapons in the school and the searches that go along with them. But we haven't talked about my single biggest criminal problem at Platt High School. Now I realize that some schools' biggest complaint is fighting or drug abuse, but not mine. Any guesses? No, not Unlawful Possession of Gravestones. My single biggest criminal problem at the high school was stealing. That's right. Good old-fashioned larceny.

When I started my first year at Platt High School, the first few months were pretty much interspersed with an equal amount of violations (fighting, threatening, stealing, etc.). But shortly thereafter, I noticed a spike in thefts that continued for some time.

What frustrates me the most is that I don't understand why it happens. How can so many students have such little respect for other people's property? There were some days when I took four theft reports in one day. Four! That's ridiculous. I never got four theft reports in one day when I worked patrol, and that was for a city of 60,000 people! Here, I was in a public school of 1,000 students and I sometimes got four reports a day. How can anyone explain that?

The fact that larceny was so prevalent at my high school made me apply a zero-tolerance policy to that crime, too. I'll freely admit, my arrest to theft ratio used to be abominable and probably my most embarrassing statistic. But after a couple of years in the school, I realized that there were several plans I could implement to try and reduce the incidence of theft.

Believe it or not, I'm going to mention rapport yet again. Befriending students and talking to them on their level is the quickest way to gain their trust and support. My students paid me back by letting me know what they knew about the thefts, if anything, and whom they suspected. I was able to make several larceny arrests based on the help of CSIs and other concerned students.

My arrest rate could have been even higher if not for the kindheartedness of several students. These students who were victims of theft made it clear to me that they did not want to press charges if the items were found; rather, they just wanted the items returned to them.

Now when I say my arrest rate could have been higher, I don't mean to sound like I'm trying to look good and get as many arrests in the school as possible. You've already read that I do not get pleasure out of arresting students that I see everyday, and I've compared it to like arresting a kid brother or sister. However, due to the severe theft problem in the school, I believed it was necessary to send a message that such criminal behavior would not be tolerated. After all, what kind of message is being sent to the student body when they find out that the only punishment they receive when they're caught stealing is that they have to give the item back to the rightful owner? Not a very strict penalty.

Another tool I used to fight the theft problem was the *School Cop* software that I mentioned earlier. I would map the areas where the thefts took place and try to find a pattern of some sort. If I were to find a pattern, it would lead me to believe that a certain person or small group of people were responsible for the thefts in that area. But of course my theft incidents were scattered throughout the school in no particular order. And they really did occur anywhere in the building: locker rooms, the cafeteria, classrooms, lockers, pool area, gymnasium, and even the nurse's office. Just imagine, you can't even get sick without worrying about your items being taken!

If a student's items were not tied down or locked away, they were as good as gone. The saddest thing about the whole matter is that whenever I made my classroom presentations to students I would emphasize the fact that theft was the biggest problem at the school and that all lockers should have locks (that work) on them and no student should ever leave their items unattended for even a short amount of time. Unfortunately, only a few students heeded my advice because the majority of kids who came to me to report a theft would admit that they didn't have a lock on their locker, or they just left their items unattended in the locker rooms.

There was no single item that was stolen more than any other. I found that all items were up for grabs. Items reported stolen to me included textbooks, money, jewelry, clothing, sneakers, purses, wallets, cellular/digital phones, backpacks, CDs and CD players, and just about anything else you can think of.

It's important to remember that each school's SRO has his own primary problem or concern. Theft just happened to be mine. Being able to identify what the top problem is will give the SRO a starting point on determining the characteristics of some of the students at the school. For example, a school with a great deal of fighting would appear to have an anger problem amongst its students. A large theft problem tells me that many students don't have respect for others. It also tells me that many students may be from low-income families and want to have items that they see their peers with, but they can't afford to go out and buy them.

Thefts, drug possession, fights...like it or not, these are the situations that come with most public high schools. But remember, school is just a microcosm of society, and stealing, drug abuse, and fighting are daily occurrences in any city. And, just like in society, sometimes police are exposed to strange and out-of-the-ordinary calls in school.

In 2001, I arrested a juvenile at Platt High School for passing a counterfeit twenty-dollar-bill in the lunch line. (You can't make this stuff up.) Also in 2001, during Christmas vacation, two students broke into the second floor of the school and forced open a file cabinet filled with field-trip money. They took the cash and burned the checks. Although a few days later they broke in again to return the cash, they had already damaged school property and trespassed during late night hours. Thanks to my relationship with the student body, I had two students who approached me and said that they had information regarding the burglary. Within a matter of weeks I had arrest warrants typed up for the students involved. They were subsequently arrested and expelled.

The case described above is significant in the fact that if the school didn't have an SRO, the chances of the students being caught and prosecuted would have been extremely slim. No doubt police would have still responded to the school to take the initial report, but without the inside information, rapport, and trust that an SRO has with his students, a detective would have been hard pressed to have solved the crime.

Around this same time I became aware of the identities of a pair of students that were involved in another incident. The incident itself was a senior prank that had happened about six months earlier. In fact, it was quite clever and funny and I would probably not have pursued the matter had it not been such a costly financial matter for the school.

On August 19, 2001, I was working day shift patrol during the summer recess. I took a drive by Platt High School and noticed the car in front of me pull over to the side of the road. A woman got out of the car and ran onto the front lawn of the school with a camera in hand. This immediately drew my attention since the school was empty and it was a Sunday morning. I was just about to ask the woman what she was doing when I looked in the direction of where she pointed the camera. My head actually did a double take at what I saw. Instead of seeing the school's full name and title ORVILLE H. PLATT HIGH SCHOOL on the front, main, outside wall about twenty feet high, I saw the words I LOVE POT HIGH.

I'll freely admit that I had a very good laugh when I saw that. Right there in large metal letters for all the world to see was the prank of a few students who actually had enough time to figure out what phrase they could make out of their school's name. And then there was the question of how they did it. The letters in question were bolted to the outside brick wall and were spring released. Did the pranksters use ladders and take each letter down, thereby having to move the ladder every time they wanted to remove the next letter? Or did they go on the roof and hang from above and remove the letters that way?

By the time I had finished the investigation, I had applied for two arrest warrants for the seniors involved. The school insisted on pursuing the matter since each letter was valued at about $100, and the remaining letters that were not used in the phrase I LOVE POT HIGH were stolen. All in all, the total monetary damage including missing letters and installation of new letters came to a little over two thousand dollars. (By the way, both seniors were arrested and, in case you're wondering, they used regular garden hoes wrapped with duct tape and removed the letters while they were on top of the roof.)

So far I've given examples of routine SRO experiences (fights, thefts, etc.) and more serious investigations (burglary, costly vandalism). But what about the emergency situations? And what about being faced with the unpleasant task of having to investigate a teacher for inappropriate and illegal behavior? These types of scenarios are covered in the following chapter.

Serious Incidents

Tuesday, September 11, 2001. I was in my police cruiser driving somewhere when my wife called me on my cell phone to tell me what happened. By the time I returned to the school, TVs were on everywhere. The rest of the day was very surreal. Not only did I have to cope with my own personal feelings knowing that our country was thrust into a national emergency, but I knew that I also had to keep my professional composure for everyone else, especially the students.

Anyone who works in a high school can attest that news travels fast in the building. If a student sneezes in a classroom at the south end of a corridor, a student will know about it in a classroom in the north end. The attacks began at 8:46 a.m., and by 10:00 a.m. every single person in the school knew about them. And that was before any official announcement by Principal Gaffney.

On that day, I saw a vulnerable, scared youth. As I stood in the hallways during pass time I watched and listened to the students as they went from one class to another. Some students asked me if they were going to die. I told them they weren't. Other students were crying. Still others I overheard discuss the possibility of being drafted. I didn't take any criminal reports that day; not because I didn't want to, but because none were reported to me—not even a theft. The students were not disrespecting teachers or each other. Everyone (including myself) was shocked over the events involving the four hijacked planes.

Parents were beginning to arrive at the school to take their children out early. Although it did not create a major problem, it was enough of a distraction to keep me from talking to students and reassuring them that they were safe.

The same could not be said for my friend and colleague Officer Sal Nesci at Maloney High School across town. Somehow a rumor developed that there was a man with a gun in or around the school. Amazingly, this rumor traveled from Maloney to Platt High School since I found out about it from parents and students in my school. There was even talk that a local radio station had gotten a hold of the rumor and broadcast it on the air, although this was never substantiated. Officer Nesci had been swarmed with parents converging on the school and pulling their kids out. While I had only about ten to twenty students removed, Sal had upwards of fifty.

By the end of the day, worry and fear had grown into animosity and anger. Students began using anti-Arab comments and slurs. Even teachers were being accused of mistreating several students of Arab descent.

September 11 was a day like no other in my career as a school resource officer. Although I have nothing to compare it with since I've been working in schools, I could only guess that the closest analogy would be the Challenger disaster or JFK's assassination. But even those events did not have students questioning if they were going to die.

Hopefully no person will ever have to go through that type of crisis again. In that type of situation, everyone must pull together and put their own emotions on the back burner for the good of the students. At Platt High School, the teachers, administrators, counselors, and paraprofessionals all came together and did an outstanding job in minimizing the shock of the events. I'm sure SROs across the country put on their counselor hats that day and did their best to control the situations in their respective schools.

September 11 was an emergency situation not just to Platt High School but to American society in general. And again, like society, schools would be subject to the same type of incidents. Several weeks after the events of 9/11, I was sitting down at my house on my lunch break when Principal Gaffney called my cell phone. "Mark," he said, "we have a student in the nurse's office who was sitting in the library going through a brochure when she got some white powder on her fingers. She's not sure what it is. I'm sure it's nothing but with all that's been going on..."

Why me?

I told him that I'd be right down. On the way back to the school I applauded myself for thinking ahead. Two weeks earlier the police chief had released a new General Order on how to respond to a biochemical threat. Fortunately I made an extra copy and kept it in my cruiser just in case such an incident occurred at the school. I remember thinking to myself that I'm a school resource officer and that I'm not supposed to get these types of calls. When I signed up for the SRO position, the last thing I thought I'd have to deal with was anthrax. And now here I was responding back to Platt High for a female student who had white powder on her fingers. That's when it hit me. I've got nothing to complain about. She can't exactly be the most upbeat person in the world right now.

When I arrived at the school, I simply followed the General Order guidelines until we were able to resolve the situation. I had a supervisor and the fire department respond to the school and we were finally able to conclude—after numerous telephone calls—that the powder from the catalogue was offset printing powder which is not at all uncommon in the printing industry. The powder is used for drying ink and reducing static electricity. Though the incident thankfully turned out to be harmless, it was nevertheless quite an experience.

The school day of September 11 and the anthrax scare that followed were days that I pray I never have to repeat. However, believe it or not, they were not my most stressful days.

In April 2002, I became embroiled in an investigation of a possible sexual relationship between a male teacher and a female student. Rumors had been circulating throughout the school about these two, but I knew them both quite well and paid little attention to the innuendo since that type of talk is common in the school setting. Additionally, I knew the teacher very well. We played basketball together several times and I considered him a friend.

Several days earlier, the teacher had approached me and asked me to clear his name from the rumors. He said (rightfully so) that this type of rumor could be very damaging and could even cost him his career if not put to a rest. I told him I understood and that I would do everything in my power to find out who's starting the gossip and put an end to it.

Then things turned for the worse.

As I began the inquiry, I became aware of evidence that substantiated the rumor. As more and more proof came out that my friend could be guilty of this serious offense, I could not help but think that I did not sign up for this kind of stress. I thought that an SRO position would consist of building rapport with students, breaking up fights, the occasional drug arrest, and classroom presentations. How was it that such serious episodes were happening at my school? I began wondering how schools managed to survive before SROs were placed in the buildings.

To make a long story short, I ended up bringing all my findings of the teacher/student affair to detectives in the Sex Crimes Unit. They took over the case, and before long an arrest warrant had been approved for the teacher. He resigned from his position when the facts were discovered and he turned himself in to police for processing.

That, too, was a trying time for the school. I felt like a traitor to the teachers in the school. I was worried that they would feel that I was coming after them and that they would begin treating me as if I was the bad guy. I don't think I could really blame them because the investigation was so secretive. Besides myself, no one knew the full story except for the school administrators and the people involved. Many teachers and students did not believe the charges and kept saying how terrible it was that the teacher was being charged. Again, if they knew what I knew, they would probably not have had that attitude.

Then again, some people who were familiar with the case and believed the allegations still felt that the charge was too harsh. They argued that the only reason the teacher was in trouble was because he was a teacher and the victim was a student. After all, the relationship was consensual. Both parties liked each other. The student was not underage (she was 18). Indeed, if this type of relationship had taken place without the teacher-student label it would hardly draw a whisper. The teacher was only in his mid-twenties so the two could have been a very common couple. However, under Connecticut state law, as in other states, any sexual relationship between student and teacher is illegal. Not only is it illegal, but it is a felony too. And as a sworn member of a municipal police department I could not turn a blind eye to a felonious crime.

The investigation of that incident depressed me for a few days. I knew I had done the right thing, but I felt that the students and teachers would now see me in a different light and regard me as a turncoat. Especially since they weren't aware of the whole story. I was fortunate enough that the week of April vacation was only days away when the incident hit the newspapers and television. Reporters tried to come on school grounds and get comments but the principal made it clear that he didn't want them on campus, which was my sentiment too. I really needed a break from that exhaustive and discouraging case. I used my compensatory and vacation time and took off April recess, as well. It was a much needed respite.

The above-listed crises are rare occurrences and probably will never happen to most school resource officers. Just as some SROs have had shootings in their schools, my stated emergencies are (hopefully) once-in-a-career events. For those of you aspiring to be a school resource officer, please be aware that I did not list the above examples to dissuade your plans. I simply believe that it is crucial that you know what you are getting yourself into. So many times I heard patrolmen talk about possibly joining the SRO ranks. Most would make great SROs, but then there are those who think that it's a walk in the park and a cushy alternative to patrol work. Those who possess that type of attitude end up hurting the students that they represent.

My experience as a school resource officer has shown me that an SRO's job is just as stressful as a patrolman's. Anyone who argues that statement has never been an SRO. Having performed both duties, I believe that I'm qualified to make that statement. I would add, however, that the stress is a different kind of stress. An SRO's stress is more of a feeling of dealing with the same people everyday. And having 1,000 students depend on you for all their legal (and sometimes non-legal) needs can be very trying. Also, an SRO does not normally have backup or another officer with whom to discuss an important decision.

A patrolman's stress is more of an anxiety type of stress. Responding to a robbery in progress, discharging a weapon, or engaging in a pursuit. Those types of stresses are adrenaline-oriented and very powerful. Yet the patrolman has an opportunity to ease out of those stresses. Once the hot call is over, he's back to responding to alarms and barking dog complaints. An SRO does not have the peaks and valleys of stress like a patrolman. Rather, he has a constant pressure to perform his duty in the same building with the same people day in and day out.

*   *   *

What happened between the teacher and student from the above example was at the very least inappropriate. Teachers should know their boundaries and never compromise their positions as the guardians of our children. But when things do go bad and these kinds of relationships are discovered, it only adds to the growing paranoia of opposite-sex encounters.

Some male teachers refuse to be alone in the same room with a female student. That's clearly their prerogative. Many police officers feel the same way. I've heard quite a few of my male colleagues say that they refuse to transport a female in their cruiser absent emergency circumstances. Again, to each his own. But my personal belief is that I'm going to treat everyone the same.

Because I initially lacked an office at the school, I usually interviewed students in areas where other people were located. However, there were often times when I needed to speak to the student privately either because the student requested it or because the topic of conversation was just too sensitive. When this was the case, I didn't hesitate to find an empty room and speak to the student alone. Some people told me I was crazy for doing that, especially with female students, but I really believe that the one-on-one conversation is key to establishing trust, rapport, and confidence.

I've talked to many students in both types of scenarios and I've noticed that students open up much more on a one-on-one level. If

I was talking to a student with an assistant principal or another teacher, the student felt like he was being double-teamed, and he shut down much more easily.

My philosophy was that if a female student (or nowadays, male for that matter) was going to accuse me of improprieties, she would do it no matter how careful I was. The main point of false accusations is that they are false. A student can come up with any lie and say that a teacher or SRO was fondling her. She doesn't actually need to meet with the adult to make up a story. To be sure, the fact that the two were alone would make the matter harder to disprove, but at the same token, it would also make it difficult to prove.

I honestly didn't worry about false female accusations. To do so would have interfered with my work as an SRO. My feeling was, if it happens, it happens. I knew in my heart that I could never take advantage of a student like that. To me, that's all that really mattered.

But you can be sure that accusations do happen.

An SRO colleague of mine, Officer Joe Vitale of the Cheshire Police Department, in Cheshire, CT, was the victim of one such false accusation. Cheshire is an affluent town bordering Meriden's west end. A female student accused him of inappropriateness and the local papers went wild with the story. Joe was taken out of the school until the investigation was finished. I found out about the accusation by reading it in the newspaper. I only knew Joe from the classes we attended together and just from those meetings I could tell that he would never do anything wrong. He's that nice of a guy.

Of course, the investigation not only came up with no evidence, but it also proved that the female student was lying. You see, the place where she said the incident occurred was monitored by school cameras. She did not know this, and the video helped disprove her claims and landed her an arrest for filing a false report.

Deciding whether or not to interview students of the opposite sex alone is a personal choice. Obviously in today's society people should be wary of their behavior around minors. The choice is up to you. I'm just one of those people who believe that if you do nothing wrong, than you've got nothing to worry about.

As you've seen from my example of the teacher who was arrested, any feelings that are acted upon, whether consensual or not, can lead to career ruin and legal damage. The distracting dress of students (whether good or bad) is one reason why I am a staunch supporter of student uniforms. While I understand that I am a police officer and not an education official, I feel that I've been exposed to the school system long enough to know a good idea when I hear one. Not only would uniforms eliminate the provocative dress of females—and males—but it would also cut down on the competitive nature of the students to see who is wearing the better clothing or better brand labels.

Many teachers agree that uniforms are the way to go. But for now most boards of education are satisfied to leave things status quo and not mandate uniforms. As I mentioned earlier, students cannot wear clothing that is disruptive to the educational process. But as we all know, that is a very subjective clause.

All this talk of dealing with students of the opposite sex and the possible perils that follow can make a person paranoid. Another instance where this discussion comes into play is whenever an SRO gives a student a ride home.

As a general rule, I did not give students rides home. That, however, didn't stop them from asking. I can't count the number of times that students approached me after school and asked for a ride home. I decided when I first took the position that I would not give students rides to their houses for several reasons. First, it would take too much time away from my other duties. Second, if I started to give one student a ride home, word of mouth would reveal that I was a new form of transportation for students and I would be inundated with requests. Third, I didn't like the idea of being away from the school in case I was needed for an emergency. And yes, I also axed the notion because of liability issues. Although I'm not one to be intimidated by frivolous lawsuits, I could not argue with the fact that by giving more students rides to their houses, I increased my chances of liability.

So you see, I explained to the students right at the beginning of each year that my car says "police" on the doors, not "taxi."

There are, however, exceptions to the rule. Obviously, if I arrested a student in the school, I transported him to the police station. Also, you've already read about "Operation: Sidewalk" and how I would bring juvenile students home to their parents if I caught them in the road. But there were also times when the school would ask me to bring a student home in the middle of the school day. For example, whenever a student was suspended during the school day and phone contact could not be made with the parent to come and pick up the child, the administration would ask me to bring the students home. Another example would involve the student's attire. There are often times when the school administrators force a student to go home and change their clothing. Occasionally, I was asked to provide the transportation.

Regardless of the student's sex, I have no problem with the request. Some officers I spoke to were worried about being accused of doing something inappropriate and refused to transport unless they were accompanied by another adult. To me, that is just ridiculous. Two adults needed to transport one child just shows how paranoid and out of control societal thinking has become.

Obviously I can't argue the fact that there are people who do terrible things to children thereby causing such paranoia. But I refuse to have my hands tied because of such degenerates. Ultimately the decision is yours whether you allow yourself to be placed in a situation that could lead to a false accusation.

* * *

Another tragic incident that a school resource officer may encounter is the death of a student. My first experience with the loss of a student came during my third year at the school. Marty Wilson was a sixteen-year-old junior at the school and was rushed to the hospital after he was struck by a car while riding his bicycle over the weekend. A couple of days later he succumbed to his injuries. Incredibly, Maloney High School across town lost a student of its own on the very same weekend. The odds of that happening are astronomical.

Wilson was well liked by students and faculty. He was a nationally ranked amateur boxer and was also well versed in martial arts. Unlike many of his contemporaries, he showed respect to everyone he came into contact with.

I knew Wilson quite well. During my first year at the school, I had a run-in with him when he got himself into some trouble. Ever since that time, he was nothing but a good student. Whenever I saw him in the hallways I would always approach him and ask him how he did in his last fight and when his next bout would be. He always shook my hand and smiled, thanking me for my interest.

Wilson's death was a shock to the student body. Fortunately, most students found out about his death through the evening news, word of mouth, or the next morning's newspaper. Had everyone found out about it during the school day, I'm sure many students would have been inconsolable and there would have been quite a few departures from the building.

Since most students had already heard the news prior to coming to school the next day, it allowed them to grieve at home with friends and families in a way that would not disrupt the school climate. It also allowed the school to be prepared for the students' arrival. Additional counselors were on hand to lend support and rooms were set up to accommodate the grief stricken.

Overall, I thought the school handled the situation as best as they could. I saw several students crying in the halls and one student showed me a poem that he had written as a tribute to Wilson. Wilson's locker became a memorial and was adorned with flowers, notes, and mementos. An outside wall of the school even became the victim of vandalism as a large Wilson tribute was drawn on the bricks. Under the depressing circumstances, the school declined to investigate and simply washed off the graffiti a few days later.

Wilson's wake brought out the entire school community. When I attended it, I saw students and teachers alike. The receiving line actually ran out the door of the funeral home. It was nice to see the school community pull together, but it's too bad that it took such a tragic incident to form the bond. Even students who I knew were enemies attended the wake and put their differences aside in respect for Wilson. If only they could show such maturity everyday.

The death of a student is just one more instance of where an SRO has to put on a different hat and be a counselor for those students who need help coping with the sadness. Adolescence is a tough enough time. Having to deal with the death of a friend is just added stress that teenagers should not have to go through.

In my estimation, it took the students about a week to get over their grief and the loss of their fallen comrade. I'm sure that internally it took much longer, but as far as seeing any visible signs of anguish and sorrow, the student body seemed to heal after a week.

Tragic and sad events are a part of life, and as a result they enter our schools as well. With the right staff on hand, students can come to grips with the harsh realities that sometimes creep into their lives. As a school resource officer, you are an essential component in the counseling scheme. Since many students feel very comfortable with their SRO, he or she will be the first one they turn to when they need explanations, comfort, or advice.

Any school resource officer can attest that the three main functions of an SRO are law enforcement, counseling, and teaching. These three facets frequently come into play all in the same day. But when dealing with the death of a student, it is painfully clear that the SRO must put his counseling skills on the front burner.

ALLIES OF THE SRO

An SRO's biggest single ally is the school principal. This should go without saying since the principal is the leader and head of the school. Although he may be subordinate to the school superintendent, he has a vast amount of powers when it comes to running the school.

A principal and a school resource officer who do not get along is a recipe for disaster. A common vision must be established between the two for the betterment of the school environment. You, as an SRO, will be able to gauge your assigned principal within the first few weeks. If you're assigned to a school and haven't heard from your principal in a few days even though he's in the school, there's a problem. An SRO should not be receiving information about serious incidents that occurred days earlier from informative teachers.

When Officer Mike Lane (the SRO at Washington Middle School across town) was first assigned to his school, he would on occasion complain that the administration sometimes would not notify him of incidents that would normally require police involvement. Such examples of isolation do no good for either party involved. There is no question that some, but not most, principals feel threatened when a police officer is assigned to their school. After all, a cop has quite a bit of power, too. A principal does not want to lose any of his authority or for that matter share it with a newcomer that is not even a school employee.

And can you blame him? For a cop, it would be like having an English teacher assigned to the police department to review reports. The teacher has no police experience, yet he is all of the sudden thrust into the police department. I can definitely understand why certain principals and teachers would have second thoughts when it comes to assigning an officer to a school.

Principals have a great amount of leverage and can be the difference between a positive SRO program and an ineffective one. A supportive principal will be open to your suggestions and willing to discuss issues with you in a collaborative manner. Initially, I had the unusual position of having a supportive principal interlaced with a board of education that had its suspicions. (The Board has since gotten much better.) Platt High School's principal, Tim Gaffney, is very fond of the SRO program. In fact, I will never forget the comment he made to me stating that if the SRO program were ever dismantled, he would leave the school. I felt this was the greatest compliment I could ever receive and that it was a result of the success of the program in his school.

Principal Gaffney always supported my ideas, too. In 2002, I had an idea for a program to help me become even more familiar with the student body. I called it the Ride-Along Police Program (RAPP) and it involved taking interested students out each day for an hour in my cruiser for a mini-patrol tour.

When I told Principal Gaffney about my idea he thought it was a great concept. And he was right. It ended up being very successful. (I'll go into greater detail about RAPP in an upcoming chapter.)

Gaffney would always let me know when there was a serious situation. He never hid anything from me. He frequently would hand me notices of upcoming training dates for school related issues. In fact, we even attended a few together.

Gaffney also let me know that if there was anything I ever needed in terms of tools or technology that he could always hold a special school drive for me to raise the money. Although I never had to take him up on his offer, I felt that this was the type of generosity and support that leads to a successful SRO program.

I was lucky. I ended up with a supportive principal. Some welcome the police. Others feel threatened or slighted, believing that the only reason the SRO was placed there is because the school has a problem.

Officer Sal Nesci (as you should know by now if you've been paying attention) was the school resource officer of Francis T. Maloney High School in Meriden, CT. His SRO career began on the same day as mine.

He was not welcomed in the school.

At the time of Nesci's placement in the school, the principal of Maloney High School was Dr. Gladys Labas. She felt that she did not need an SRO in her school and was against the idea of having one assigned to her. (The SRO program was the result of a federal grant that was agreed upon by the Meriden Police Department and the Board of Education. The school principals didn't really have a choice.)

→ all for money

Fast forward to September 2002. Dr. Labas may very well have become the staunchest supporter of the program. She did a complete about-face and ended up using Officer Nesci as much as possible. She complimented him constantly and even pushed to provide him an office! Of course the superintendent shot that down.

Nesci himself deserved much of the credit. A very personable officer, he showed that he could get along with anyone, in addition to being a great speaker and investigator. Due to his diligence and positive effects at the school, he was able to turn a negative situation of not being wanted into a state of cooperation and helpfulness.

One thing that is common among principals who support their SROs is that once they have their officers in the school, they don't want them to leave for an extended period of time. In other words, administrators do not like when SROs take vacation time during the school year or when the police department sends SROs to training classes for weeks at a time. The schools have become so dependent on SROs that they really frown upon days when the officer is not available. Can you argue with this thinking? If the SRO is doing an effective job and helping the school, it's only normal that the administration would want him there as much as possible.

As far as vacations are concerned, there's really no reason (barring any unforeseen circumstance) why a school resource officer should take any time off when school is open. I always took my vacations at the same time that the students and teachers did. In my school district the students have a week off at Christmas time, in February, and in April. Then, of course, there is the summer break. These are usually the times when I used my vacation days. Otherwise, if I took time off while school was in session, not only would I be shortchanging the school, but I would have to revert back to patrol work while school was out of session.

The training issue is another point of contention for administrators. I already mentioned how training classes became more prevalent once I became an SRO. Obviously that was a plus for me, but the school administration soon began to dread whenever I was sent to a new class. Principal Gaffney, as well as the other city principals, understood that updated training was important, but they didn't like that it took away from my time at the school. At one point, during our semiannual police/board of education meetings, Gaffney asked if SRO training could be withheld until the summer months when school is no longer in session. Lt. Thorp, the SRO commander, explained that police training comes on a first come, first serve basis, and that it must be taken at the time of announcement or it may pass by.

I understand the principals' reluctance to give up their SROs for days, sometimes even weeks, at a time. At the same time, I feel that constant training is necessary and helpful to the school resource officer. I have attended many classes that the police department has sent me to and I've gained significant knowledge of facts and ideas that I previously did not know.

Again, Officer Muir would cover my school when I was unavailable. Most SROs don't have the luxury of having another officer next door. For them, balancing the time between training classes and being in the school can be more of a problem. Only through open communication among the administrators and the SRO can a compromise be reached in which both the school and the officer benefit.

Another point to constantly keep in mind is that the principal is the boss. He's not *your* boss, but he is in charge. There are not many instances where the SRO can take over, but they do exist. One such instance is when the school becomes a crime scene. Anytime that a serious criminal incident occurs at a school (e.g., school shooting, major accident, suicide, etc.) the police take over. A good rule of thumb to remember is that public safety outweighs everything. Whenever public safety becomes jeopardized in or around the school, the police take over. Period. The police were in charge at Columbine, not the principal. School administrators are extremely educated and know everything there is to know about their school. They are not trained to deal with a serious shooting. The police department is. If someone wants to find out what is involved in a PPT (Planning and Placement Team) conference or what the requirements are for eligibility for special education services they are not going to ask an SRO. Or at least they shouldn't.

If a student starts shooting up a gymnasium and throwing pipe bombs down the hallway, the principal is no longer running the show. The police respond and the police take over.

Another case where an SRO can overrule a principal is when a bomb threat is called in to the school. However, rational judgment must be used here. Generally, when a bomb threat is called in, the principal makes the decision of whether to evacuate the building or not. The SRO should make a scan of the building with custodians since they know the building better than just about anyone. Any findings are then reported to the principal who makes the choice. HOWEVER...if for some justifiable reason the SRO feels that this particular threat is for real and may cause harm to the students in the building, he does have the right to overstep the principal and order the evacuation of the building.

This call by the SRO should only be executed if he has a good reason to do so and honestly believes that public safety is at risk. Even then it is a good idea to contact a police supervisor and talk it over with him before making the final decision.

It is important to remember that the SRO is there to assist the principal, not direct him. An SRO with the latter kind of attitude will find himself back on patrol faster than you can say "10-4."

The relationship between a principal and SRO is a crucial one. If the two cannot get along, then the school will suffer and the school resource officer program will not be a productive one. On the other hand, the combination of a supportive principal and an enthusiastic SRO will result in positive benefits to the entire school community.

* * *

A principal's job is never-ending: administrative paperwork, meetings with staff and superintendents, coordinating school functions, interviewing and hiring employees, keeping up with current education policies, taking calls from all types of parents. It's quite a load.

Enter the assistant principal. Ladies and gentlemen, this is the person with whom you will probably be working the most. You see, in most schools the assistant principal is in charge of discipline. The assistant principal greatly alleviates the head principal from having the pressure of dealing with disciplinary action in addition to his already full schedule.

Schools differ in the amount of assistant principals they have. Some have none. Others have six or more. Platt High School has two assistant principals. When I began my SRO career, the assistant principals were Joseph Paluszewski and Greg Shugrue. Here again I lucked out. Joe and Greg are two great guys who supported me wholly. We had a mutual kind of respect for each other seeing that we usually dealt with the same students over and over.

The two assistant principals are responsible for any disciplinary action to all students in the school. That's about 500 students per assistant principal. Greg dealt with students whose last name began with letters A-L, and Joe took M-Z. Since I frequently assisted them, I ended up dealing with A-Z.

They both had their share of problem students and, from what I've seen, were equally good in their work. Joe and Greg knew how to utilize me. They never overused or underused me. I've spoken to some SROs who complained that their assistant principal(s) call them for every little thing. No matter how small the discipline, the assistant principal will call to have the SRO present: "Sally, I told you that spaghetti straps are not allowed in the school." What is an SRO supposed to do in this situation? He can't do anything more than what the assistant principal is already doing. In fact, he probably can't even do that much since the violation is one of school policy.

Interestingly enough, this again brings up the question of how an SRO enforces school rules. Of course, this is another example of school discretion. As I've already stated, I've met a few school resource officers who are allowed to discipline students. These SROs can give students detentions and apply other punishments to them. However, from most of the SROs I've met, this is not the norm.

Most SROs leave the discipline to the assistant principals. So did I. If I were in the school and witnessed a school violation (such as a student smoking or wearing inappropriate clothing) I would send the student to the main office and advise the proper assistant principal. I didn't step on their toes and they didn't step on mine. When an SRO has two knowledgeable assistant principals like Greg and Joe, it only makes the working relationship that much smoother.

Greg and Joe called on me whenever there was a criminal violation or when they believed that one would occur. They also had me sit in with them on mediations between students who didn't like each other. The assistant principal explained the penalty for fighting and violating the school's rule, and then I explained the criminal penalties of the fight.

Assistant principals also have great leverage in the school and can help make an SRO's job more effective. Case in point: During my first two years at Platt High School, students were allowed to mill around the building until 3:00 p.m., one hour past the end of the school day. I quickly realized that this was not a good idea since students could go just about anywhere in the building and not be supervised. I'm sure this also contributed to the theft problem at the school.

After discussing the problem with the administrators they decided to open the 2002/2003 school year with a new rule and announcement. Greg had told the school secretary to make two announcements: one at 2:20 p.m. and the other at 2:30 p.m. The first gave any remaining students in the building a reminder that the school would be closed in ten minutes and that no one should be in the building after that time. The final announcement at 2:30 indicated that the school was now closed and no students should be in the building without permission.

I cannot explain enough how effective this simple announcement had changed the after-school environment. Not only did it totally empty the school of unnecessary students, but it also gave me the power to issue tickets to any stragglers who chose to stay. By having the school secretary announce daily that no one was allowed in the building after 2:30, any student who ignored that broadcast could be accused of trespassing.

Another issue that SROs and assistant principals need to examine is...the law. I've heard stories from many an SRO where an assistant or head principal wants a student arrested, yet the SRO cannot perform the deed because no law has been broken.

SROs cannot arrest students for insubordination or school violations unless a law has been broken as well. Acquainting school administrators with the penal code will help avert any situation where an administrator requests that a student be arrested, especially if the school official makes the request in the presence of the student. Such an instance happened to me in my first year as a school resource officer. I had arrested a student for possession of

127

marijuana and during the search of his person I discovered a folding knife. One of the principals wanted me to charge the student with possession of a dangerous weapon. I told him that I could only do that if the blade portion of the knife was four inches or longer in length. We measured the knife and it came out to be only three and three-quarters inches in length. The principal was not happy that I couldn't charge the student, but I knew that I had no choice. My state's statute had no charge for the possession of a knife that was under four inches in length.

Just as it is beneficial to have school administrators review penal law (or at least have it explained to them), it is just as practical to have the SRO review school law. When I first entered my assigned high school I was totally uninformed as to what rights students, teachers, and administrators had. I highly recommend all SROs to study their respective state's education laws. After going over Connecticut's school laws, I became much more comfortable in my role at the school and how to combine my police powers with the authority of school officials.

Good assistant principals will know how to work hand-in-hand with their SRO. They will know how to better handle a problem student using school discipline or law enforcement. With the combination of those two punitive choices, schools have more firing power to deal with obnoxious, disrespectful, and criminal behavior.

I know it's hard to believe, but not all students are angels. We're not in Kansas anymore, Toto. Gangs have infiltrated schools for years now. Students freely talk back, swear, and even verbally abuse teachers and administrators. Drugs are dealt in the hallways and bathrooms. Weapons are brought into the building. On good days these types of students are manageable. On bad days they are out of control and an SRO is kept busy. Fearing litigation, teachers are scared to put their hands on students even when it is clearly warranted.

School administrators used to be the only people who kept the school from becoming chaotic. I think it's now safe to add school resource officers to that list. And when principals and SROs work together it's a powerful combination. As long as these two groups continue to work side by side for the common good of the school, harmful and negative students will not be able to thrive in the educational environment.

*   *   *

I love teachers. Heck, I'm married to a teacher. I honestly believe that the majority of people don't know the dedication that these people put into their work. Teachers have one of the most thankless jobs in the world, along with policemen. I've seen people in both these professions do so much good only to be mistreated or taken for granted by the ones they serve.

Obviously not all citizens are unaware of the devotion that teachers show. But there are, amazingly, enough people out there who think that teachers are nothing but glorified babysitters.

I remember reading an article somewhere that satirized a letter from a fictional woman who was angry over the pay that teachers made and felt that they should be paid on the same scale as baby sitters since that is essentially what they are, in her opinion.

She began by saying that a $50,000 salary is a ridiculous amount for a teacher to make for simply "watching" kids during the day. She went on to recommend that teachers make $5.00 an hour. That would then be multiplied by 20 since that was an average amount of children in a classroom. That figure would then be multiplied by eight, since the teacher worked an eight-hour workday. The woman scoffed at the fact that teachers be paid during the summer or vacations and argued that they only be compensated for the 180 school days they work. The article then depicted the woman calculating the above factors to determine what a teacher's salary should be. When the total amounted to $144,000, the woman writing the letter begins to stammer and tries to find a mistake.

I have been very fortunate at Platt High School in that I got along with every teacher in the building. There are close to 100 teachers employed there and I don't have a bad thing to say about any of them. They honestly care about their jobs and the children they teach. I give them all the credit in the world.

When I was an SRO, teachers played a significant role in my job performance. By having a supportive faculty who not only accepted, but also insisted on, my presence, I was able to do my job with a confidence of knowing that we were all working together without problematic background issues.

Knowing that the teachers wanted me in the school and complimented me on my work only made me want to strive to be even better. Remember, as an SRO, I was an outsider coming into their place of work. I had no idea of what to expect. The teachers are the backbone of the school. If they don't like you, you're going to have a long, difficult road as a school resource officer. Fortunately, I didn't experience any animosity.

The compliments I received from teachers continue to this day. I appreciate them so much. For an SRO, there is nothing like being told by a veteran teacher that the school is doing so much better since the officer's arrival. When praises such as those start coming, you know that you're doing a good job.

Before July 2004, the city of Meriden had to decide whether or not to take over the funding of the SRO program (since it was initially paid for by a federal grant) or scrap it altogether. Teachers frequently asked me about the funding issue because they didn't want to lose their SRO. I was constantly flattered when they told me this and I was glad to know that my work at the school was appreciated. In fact, many teachers told me that they would not allow me to be pulled from the school and that they would sign petitions, write the local paper, or do whatever necessary to keep me at the school. With that kind of support behind me, I was only motivated to do even more positive things for the teachers and the school.

I believe the teachers liked having me at the school for several reasons. First, I think they liked me as a person and considered me a friend. I regarded many teachers as my friends and was sad when I chose to leave them. Second, the teachers have told me that they felt safer with me in the school and could concentrate more on teaching instead of worrying about violent students. Many of the teachers recalled how intense the school climate was in the early to mid-1990s when the teenage gangs were prevalent in the schools. Third, teachers were glad to see an adult in the building who had the authority to physically control a student. I recall one day when one of the assistant principals (I can't remember which one) and I were called to the area outside one of the classrooms for an unruly

131

student. As we both arrived, I saw the student (whom I was familiar with) surrounded by three or four teachers. The student wanted to leave the area but the teachers were blocking his path since he needed to be sent to the office. The teachers informed us that "Joe" was out of control, swearing at one of them, and refusing to go to the office. While the teachers were describing the incident to us, "Joe" tried to leave again. I instinctively grabbed the handle of the backpack that was on "Joe's" back and pulled him back into the group. The assistant principal and I then led him to the office.

After that incident, you would have thought I'd parted the Red Sea. The teachers who witnessed me yank "Joe" back into the group were so impressed that I could physically take control of a student that it was all they could talk about. "Officer Mark," they would say, "you did what we always dream about doing." I thanked them for their compliments, but at the same time I let them know that they, too, could have done the same thing. Teachers have every right to use physical force when necessary to control a student. But sadly, as I discussed earlier, too many teachers are intimidated by frivolous litigation to take the chance of placing their hands on students.

To a school resource officer, teachers are an important asset to school criminal investigations. Teachers know countless students and can shed insight on a particular one that may be involved in criminal activity. Teachers also frequently came to me (just as students did) with information of possible criminal activity. Many times I was advised of a student who was seen smoking a joint after school or making a threat toward another student. The teachers realized that in order for me to be effective I needed as much help as possible.

It was very difficult at first, but I made certain to learn the names of all the teachers. I wanted them to know that I respected them and what they did. I felt it was the least I could do since none of them gave me any problems when I first joined the school. However, I was very lucky. Some SROs face resistance and animosity from the school staff when they are assigned to a school although, according to many SROs, this is not commonplace. But it does happen. One school resource officer I know faced constant frigidity from a few members of the staff at a middle school. One teacher recognized the SRO from an incident that occurred a year earlier in which the teacher's relative was involved. The teacher made it clear to the officer that she was not happy with the officer's presence.

As if that wasn't enough to demoralize the SRO, a guidance counselor began to take umbrage at the fact that the officer was talking to students and giving them advice on certain issues. Apparently the counselor felt it was his job to give advice to the students and not the SRO's. This kind of thinking is laughable as a police officer's job is frequently relegated to giving advice and helping people in times of need.

Overall, most teachers have nothing but positive things to say about school resource officers. But just like anywhere else in life there will always be a small faction who cannot agree with the majority and for some reason do not agree with having a police officer in a school. Barring an unforeseen circumstance, these attitudes cannot be changed. People with these types of attitudes are usually very hypocritical when it comes to the police. It's just like when a cop works the street and runs into the scum of the earth who refer to police as "pigs" or other derogatory labels. These people claim to hate the police, but when they become victims of a crime or need some legal assistance, they still call 9-1-1.

An SRO must learn to work through these negative attitudes and continue to perform his job to the best of his ability. If these pessimists start to have an impact on the SRO's performance and demoralize his character then the whole school could suffer and miss out on all the affirmative results of the SRO program.

A true test as to whether an SRO is accepted at a school comes when the officer begins to investigate an incident involving a teacher. A school resource officer is not just responsible for student criminal behavior but for all crimes regardless of who commits them. You've already read about my investigation involving the teacher who had a sexual relationship with a student. During that entire probe I was concerned that the teachers would regard me as a traitor and think that I was "out to get them." While some teachers could not believe the accusations and stood in the suspect's corner, not one of them ever gave me a hard time for doing my job. They saw that I was in rough shape also, and that I did not enjoy investigating friends. Many teachers came up to me and told me to "hang in there," or asked me if I was okay. I was proud to know these people and glad that none of them treated me any differently even though I was partially responsible for the demise of one of their comrades. This kind of support is what allowed me to realize that I was very fortunate to be working with such an understanding faculty. Even though I realize that not every SRO has that benefit, I firmly believe that the teacher-SRO relationship is one that can make or break a school resource officer program.

Another aspect of the teacher-SRO relationship that I didn't foresee is the advice and counseling that teachers seek. When I first entered the school, I was so focused on helping the students that I overlooked the fact that teachers are human too, and have problems that *they* need assistance with.

I frequently had teachers who approached me and asked my input on certain legal issues that they were dealing with personally. They asked what they should do in certain situations such as domestic problems, or issues with their children and drugs. I've been asked my opinion on neighbor disputes, questioned about the specifics of gun laws, and inquired in regards to motor vehicle laws. I've even had a few faculty members come to me with traffic tickets that they received in hopes of having them quashed.

As for the latter issue, I'll refer you to your department's policy. I know for me that it's not worth risking my job over someone else's mistake.

School administrators and teachers are integral components of the school resource officer program. An SRO comes into contact with these educators on a daily basis and relies on them for success in his work. But there is yet another group of people that prove very helpful when dealing with students, and they have more influence than any of the previous groups mentioned.

Welcome to the wonderful world of parents.

           *   *   *

A parent is an SRO's friend. Remember that. I tried to make contact with as many parents as possible. After all, I was dealing with their children on a daily basis. I felt they should at least know what I looked like and get to know my personality.

During my first few weeks as an SRO, I came to the conclusion that many parents would be shocked if they ever saw the way their children acted in school. I've seen some students go absolutely wild on the high school campus, but then I would see the same student a few days later in the company of his mother or father and you'd think the student had a personality transplant. One female student I met during my first year at the school was constantly getting referred to the office and getting suspended. I even considered her a suspect in multiple thefts at the school but I could never get enough evidence. One day I happened to see her with her mother at the school. The student was quiet, polite, and even personable. It was a complete reversal. It was then that I discovered that many students use the school setting as an outlet so that they can let it all hang loose and go wild.

Witnessing the type of impact that parents have over their children made me realize that I needed to involve the parents more with my work and its relation to their sons and daughters.

I learned that since I was a police officer with a cruiser and not tied to the school, I could make house visits to students' homes and chat with the parents. Even teachers didn't have that luxury. Once I started to make the visits I found that the parents usually appreciated my call and said that they would deal with their child.

I recall one incident where two students were involved with a theft. Forty dollars was taken from the bag of a female student. Thanks to my confidential student informants I was quickly able to ascertain the suspects' names. Because the female student did not want to file any charges (she just wanted them to return her money), I did not arrest the boys whom I knew well and would never assume to be thieves. I did, however, notify the boys' parents in person, explaining the circumstances of the crime and how I would appreciate any help they could give me by talking to their children.

Not all parents are quick to take a law enforcement officer's word. Some parents suffer from what I call the "Not My Child" syndrome. This denial by certain parents stems from the fact that their child is a Jekyll and Hyde. The child acts one way in the home or wherever the parent is around and then lets his hair down when the parent is out of sight.

It's very difficult to change the mind of a parent who will defend his child to the end.

Recall the incident I had with the two students who broke into the school during Christmas vacation. Initially when the parents of each child responded to the school, they were shocked and disheartened to learn what their child had done. That would be the normal reaction of just about any disappointed parent. I told the parents that I would do what I could for the students since they were being cooperative. I also advised them that I would visit them within the next few days to obtain statements from the suspects so that the court could see that they were being cooperative. It didn't surprise me that when I went to get the statements from the students, their respective fathers told me that they "sought legal counsel" and were told not to give any statements.

I smiled at their responses for a couple of reasons. First, I expected them to pull this kind of stunt. Secondly, I found it humorous that the only ones they would end up hurting was themselves.

You see, I believe people should keep their words. As an SRO at Platt High School, my job hinged on my word. If I were to lie to students or misuse their trust, I would not have been very successful at the school.

When the two students admitted to me that they had burglarized the school and I could see that they were remorseful and cooperative, I told them that I would help them and only charge them with the minimum required statutes. Even though there were a couple of other crimes I could have charged them with, they were minor and unnecessary.

Unfortunately the parents took advice from their lawyer and told their kids to clam up. That was unwise on their part. I already had enough evidence to apply for the two arrest warrants so I didn't even need the written statements. The sole purpose of the students' written statements was to show the court that the boys were cooperative and remorseful. When I tell the students that I'll do what I can to help them, I mean it. It's too bad that the two fathers didn't trust me. Since they would not cooperate and allow the statements, I knew that I had to play hardball as well. I charged the boys with every applicable statute I could find and gave them no breaks whatsoever. It angered me that the parents didn't trust me and tried to make my investigation difficult. Only the boys lost out in the end. They still got arrested, only with more charges than they would have had they supplied me with their written statements. I hope the parents didn't pay that lawyer too much money.

The above example is a rare one in that it depicts uncooperative parents. For some reason parents cannot grasp that their offspring did something illegal or any kind of act that necessitated police involvement. Thankfully most parents are more realistic and know that no one is perfect. People make mistakes, including our children. And from what I've seen, parental discipline is alive and well. Think about it. What would you do if your kid got arrested or was brought home by a cop? Better yet, what would your father have done to you? I know I wouldn't be sitting for a week, and my brother officers concur the same would have happened to them.

However, there are quite a few parents who are scared to raise a hand to their child for fear of being arrested for child abuse. Here again is where I can be a resource to parents and explain that they have every right to physically discipline their children. It amazes me how many parents believe that spanking is illegal. It's just like when we talked about the teachers and their hesitance to use physical force on students. Society has become so paranoid over legal consequence that common sense has taken a back seat to fear.

It is very refreshing to me when I see a parent discipline a child. Too many times I see kids stepping all over their parents, especially their mothers. There have been a few times when I've arrested teenagers and heard them call home and address their mothers as "bitch." "Yo, bitch, come pick me up; I'm at the police station." And the mother shows up! It's mind-boggling!

Fathers are not immune either. One unbelievable story an assistant principal once told me involved a FIVE-YEAR-OLD elementary student who for one reason or another refused to get onto a school bus to go home. When a teacher came out to tell the child to get on the bus, the student still resisted. Fearing to touch the student, the teacher than called for an administrator who came across the same resistance. Finally, the school called the boy's father and asked him to take his child home. When the father arrived, the child was still being stubborn and refused to get on the bus or go with his father in the car. The school officials, waiting for the father to take his son home, were shocked when they heard him say that he couldn't physically take his son because he feared an arrest if he touched him.

Yes, you read that last line correctly. A father was scared to *touch* his son—not hit his son, mind you, but touch his son—for fear of being arrested. Are you kidding me? Can you imagine that child's life at home?! He rules the roost.

The above incident is a prime example as to why I feel contact is important with parents. As you can see, some parents are just clueless when it comes to the law. So not only is it important to keep them abreast of their children's behavior in the school, but it's also beneficial to be a resource to them and let them know what their rights are as parents.

Obviously the types of parents as those listed above are the minority, yet there are more than you would think. Nevertheless, I usually get beneficial cooperation from most of the students' parents.

One prime example involved a student we'll call "George" whom a teacher saw smoking marijuana on school property after school. I verified the teacher's account by talking to other students who witnessed the incident. I needed corroboration not because I didn't believe the teacher but because I wanted to make sure the substance being smoked was indeed marijuana and not a cigarette.

After getting confirmations of the teacher's account, I went to visit George's father at his local place of business. I asked him if he could stop by the school so that he, George, and I could all sit down together and discuss the situation. He immediately came down.

Once at the school, I called for George and the three of us had discussed what had happened and how George could face serious educational and criminal penalties for smoking marijuana on school property. The effect of the presence of George's father was nothing short of astounding.

I had dealt with George in the past and he was a wisecracking student who would push me as far as he could. He had a severe attitude problem and spent some time in the principal's office. So when I found out that I would have to speak with him, I knew I needed to take another approach. I had gotten along fine with George's father when I met him a couple of times before. His assistance in the above situation let me know I had a parent in my corner. George's dad said that George would have to face the consequences if he ever got caught doing something illegal. He said that he would support my actions and thanked me for alerting him to the problem. We shook hands and sent George back to class.

To me, that was the perfect way to handle a situation that would otherwise probably have had no effect on George if I had talked to him alone. Since that meeting with George and his father, I haven't had any additional problems with George.

As an SRO, it is important to remember that the parent/SRO relationship is a two-way street. Just as I needed assistance and involvement from parents, they too needed help from me on occasion. For example, there have been many instances when parents came to me and said that their child was having problems with another student. Usually these problems consist of bullying, harassment, or some other type of annoying yet potentially serious behavior.

When a parent comes to a school resource officer with such a problem, it is imperative that the officer investigates it to the fullest and speaks with all parties involved. A follow-up call to the parent is highly advisable, as the parent will be very grateful and willing to help the SRO when he calls that same parent for assistance in the future.

I also recommend calling parents when you recognize a significant change in the behavior of a student. In my third year at the school I noticed a male student in the eleventh grade who was starting to hang out with some real lowlifes. He was no longer on the football team as he was in the past, and he wasn't with his girlfriend anymore. Rumor around the school was that he was beginning to deal drugs and delve into other criminal activities.

Many times, parents are clueless to their children's behavior and, remarkably, are the last ones to notice any type of change. However, if a police officer suddenly appears on their doorstep one day with information that their son or daughter is clearly slipping from the social footing they once held, the parent usually will consider that to be serious enough to perform some kind of closer examination, if not interdiction, into their child's life.

An SRO that does not involve parents is only making his job harder than it needs to be. Parents are a huge factor in their children's lives and have tremendous influence. By taking the time out to go make house calls—or even telephone calls—to the parents of students, an SRO is not only making his job more effective, but also gaining a very important ally. After all, if you were a parent, wouldn't you want to know if a police officer was concerned about your child?

TOOLS OF THE TRADE

In the last chapter, I explained how certain people can affect or help you as a school resource officer. Now I would like to focus our attention on the tools and objects that can make an SRO's job more efficient and productive.

When I was sent to Platt High School on my first day as an SRO, the police department sent me there with nothing more than the same equipment I had used on patrol: my gun belt, uniform, and police cruiser. Being new to the SRO position, I didn't even expect that I would need anything else. That all changed within a few months.

The first thing that I realized I would need is a list of names of the entire student body. This list would include their full name, address, phone number, and date of birth since these were all items that I needed for my police reports. The secretaries in the main office were a huge help to me and provided me this type of list on a monthly basis since student enrollment frequently changed. This student body list was invaluable as it enabled me to confirm student ages and addresses. Believe it or not, some students would lie to me about their ages when I asked them. Having the list of every student's date of birth was crucial so that I could determine if the student was a juvenile or an adult. In Connecticut, the cutoff age is sixteen. Under that age you're considered a juvenile. Sixteen and older makes you an adult. Since the average age range in high school is fourteen to eighteen, I was dealing with both juvenile and adult students on a constant basis and needed to be sure of their correct birth date.

Addresses were crucial for a couple of reasons. Obviously, if I needed to visit the parent or student at home, I had to know where I was going. My frequent home visits were one reason why I kept a second copy of the student list in my car. I would keep one at the school and one in my cruiser so that I could refer to it in case I ever needed it outside of the building, which I often did. Too many times to count, I would encounter students during the summer months or while I was working an extra overtime shift on the weekend. Keeping a spare list in my car came in very handy.

Another reason why I needed the address listing was to make sure the student didn't live out of district. Since the city of Meriden has two public high schools, the city is divided into two districts. The district you live in determines which high school you attend. This is how many cities divide the student population. Besides convenience (by sending students to the school closest to them), this plan also tries to ensure that each school gets the proper amount of funding based on it's student population and where they live in the district. When students lie about their address and attend a school that is out of their district, the wrong school ends up getting funds.

You'd be amazed how many students and families try to pull off this scheme. Sometimes it works. Most of the time it does not. Although Platt High School has its own personnel to deal with these violations, I tried to help out whenever I became aware of a student that was living out of district.

Officer Sal Nesci and I shared frequent quips with each other whenever we sent each other out of district students. In a majority of the cases, the out of district student was usually a problem student that we were glad to send across town. Whenever Nesci found out that his high school would be transferring a problem student to Platt High School, he got on the phone and wished me luck with the student, but not before giving me a big chortle and a sigh of relief. I can't really blame Nesci because I did the same thing to him.

The listing of the student body was the first tool I needed. But I quickly realized that the student I.D. photos were almost as useful.

I honestly don't know what I would have done without the pictures of the student body that were on file in the main office. During my first year at the school, I would go through the photos and try to memorize the students' names to their faces. Once I became more familiar with the students, the pictures did not become any less significant.

Quite often I would have a student come to me with a complaint of another student whose name was not known. The complainant would supply me with a description or a nickname. If I felt I knew the person being described, I would bring out several photos, including the one I thought he was, and have the complainant pick out the student in question. In essence, I had my own little photo lineup right at the school.

*   *   *

In my four years at Platt High School, I've only been ordered out to assist with a city crisis once. It happened during my first year at the school. A male had barricaded himself inside his house with a shotgun and refused to come out. All four city SROs were told to report to the scene downtown. This was easier said than done.

As I'm sure most police officers can attest, police radios are not perfect. Some might even say they're flawed. The four SROs in Meriden (at the time Muir, Lane, Nesci, and myself) had always had trouble contacting each other and the police department via the portable police radios because they simply didn't work well inside the school buildings. Unless we were standing right next to a window, it was very unlikely that we would hear when someone was calling us.

This finally came to light on the day of the barricade. Apparently the department had been trying to reach the SROs for a while. When the four of us finally did arrive at the scene, the police chief at the time ordered that the SROs be issued department Nextel cellular phones so that they could be contacted more easily.

Personally, I was surprised that the chief did this. Not only were the cellular phones restricted to supervisors (sergeants, lieutenants, etc.), but I was sure that it would take forever to add four more phones to the current stockpile. After all, I had seen for too long how slowly a municipality takes to do certain things.

(By the way, in case you're wondering, the barricaded man ended up committing suicide.)

Amazingly, within days, the four SROs were given Nextel phones that included the Direct Connect feature. For the uninitiated, this option allows the user to use the phone as a kind of "walkie-talkie" where two people can talk to each other privately.

To this day I am grateful that the chief of police gave the SROs those phones. They were indispensable. I don't know how I did my duties before I had my phone. With it, I was able to communicate with the other SROs without tying up the patrol frequency. We could get in touch with each other regardless of where we were as the signal was much stronger than my police radio. It allowed me to get in contact with my supervisor since he carried one with him as well. If I made house calls and no one answered the door, I would double-check by using my assigned phone to call the house. Many times the resident was sleeping and the phone call woke him.

A perfect example of how the Nextel Direct Connect feature is such an asset occurred in my third year at Platt High. By that time, Officer Kristin Muir had left Lincoln Middle School on maternity leave and was replaced by Officer Steve Lespier. One particular morning, Lespier beeped me on the two-way radio portion of the phone and told me that one of his students just reported to him that he had been robbed of his gold chain while walking to school. School was just starting and Lespier gave me a description of the two high school students and the necklace. As luck would have it, I was in the main office standing by the "sign-in-late" room when Lespier relayed the information to me. I looked in the late room to find the two students who were just described to me. Not only that, but they were holding and admiring a gold necklace! I brought the students into an assistant principal's office and told Lespier to come over to my school with the victim. It was all downhill from there as the high school students were arrested and suspended.

If it weren't for the Nextel phones, Lespier's message would never have gotten to me so clearly and expeditiously. If we had still been using portable radios, Lespier would have had to wait for other officers to stop communicating. Even then, I probably would not have heard his message since the area where I was standing is sometimes a "dead spot" for radio signals.

The Nextel Direct Connect feature helped me stay in contact with SROs outside my own department, too. This is significant as it allowed me to coordinate with other SROs who may have needed information and assistance. Earlier in the book I mentioned Connecticut State Trooper Heather Ingala who was the SRO of the state-run technical school down the road from me. She and her school administrators were issued Nextel phones in her third year at the school. Ingala and the head administrator wanted to add me to their Direct Connect list so that we could be in contact in case of an emergency and due to the proximity of our respective schools. I thought this was a great idea and the three of us added each other to our phone lists.

I also liked to add any other SROs to my phone list in case I needed any help or information. Educational and criminal law are ever-changing topics. The more resources you have to obtain the information you need, the better your program will operate.

The Nextel phones were extremely beneficial to the SRO program. I strongly urge any SROs that work closely with one or more school resource officers to appeal to either their police or school administrators for purchasing these types of phones. They are well worth their price and give the program a more professional quality.

*　　　　　　　*　　　　　　　*

Depending on the school setting and climate, an SRO would probably benefit from the use of a mountain bike. During the first year of my assignment, I became aware that a police mountain bike would help my job abundantly. Platt High school is bordered to the east by woods and a dirt trail that leads south behind a row of houses and then into more woods. This path was a frequent route taken by students who skipped out of school early. Several times I've been notified by school personnel that students have left the building and were seen heading down the path. In order to locate the kids, I would either jog down the path on foot or hop into my cruiser and drive to the residential street that borders the path. The former option was not my favorite. If I elected to run down the path after the students, I started out with clean boots and usually returned with dirty ones. Also, the students would have such a vast head start over me that my chances of catching up to them were slim. A bicycle changes all that and would enable me to catch the runners.

When I jumped into my cruiser and drove down the residential street adjoining the path, I hoped that the students would come out from the path through the backyards and onto the street. Although this has worked in the past on a few occasions, many students would see my car when it started coming down the street so they just kept walking into the woods and came out another way.

Another reason that a bicycle would be beneficial is by getting the SRO closer to the students during morning arrival or afternoon dismissal. I requested a police bike from my supervisor just for this purpose. During afternoon dismissal, throngs of students come out of the building at once. It's a prime time for fights to occur. It's also the time when I had to travel down a few streets to ensure proper pedestrian conduct. I would use my patrol car to drive up and down the street to make sure everything was status quo. Although this did get the job done, it was very impersonal and cumbersome. With a bicycle, I could ride up to the students and deal with them on a more intimate level. The bike would also allow me quicker movement and turn-around capabilities than my cruiser did. For example, if I were talking to a group of students on the sidewalk and I saw a problem erupt behind them, down the walk, I would simply have to turn my bicycle in that direction and pedal to the incident. When in my car, I had to shift to reverse, back into a driveway, watch for pedestrians, and then turn toward the incident. Yes, I know it's only a few more moments, but to a student that's getting his bell rung, a few seconds means a lot.

The bicycle would accentuate the ever-important rapport building process. It would enable me to talk to the students privately, rather than over the public address system for the whole world to hear. The bike would also allow me access anywhere (e.g., backyards, woods, streams, etc.) whereas the cruiser kind of loses its usefulness once the pavement ends.

As you should know by now if you've been paying attention, Lincoln Middle School is across the street from Platt High School. When Officer Muir was the SRO at Lincoln, she would occasionally call for my assistance. To get there I would have to get into my car and drive there. Because of the design of the school, I would have to take a couple of turns and deal with a traffic light. With a bicycle, I could simply pedal out of the front door of Platt, cross the street, pedal across the playing field and arrive at the front door of Lincoln. My response time would actually be faster with a bicycle.

Any SRO who has different terrain around his school and wants to build even more rapport (again, you can never have enough) with his students should definitely look into the possibility of acquiring a police bike.

Just as in any profession, an SRO should use tools that make the job more efficient. Officer Mike Lane (the first SRO of Washington Middle School) carried around his own personal laptop computer with him, which helped facilitate his report writing and contact information. Other SROs I know use Palm Pilot's to assist with their schedules and contacts.

A good SRO will continue to strive and find new ways to make his program succeed. As times change and new technologies and tools become available, the SRO should focus on those items that will allow the program to grow as well.

*   *   *

Another tool that cannot be overlooked is a crisis plan. Also known as a critical incident booklet, this important tool sets forth certain guidelines to follow in case of an emergency or crisis situation. For a school not to have some type of crisis plan in this day and age is just plain negligent. How many attacks do we have to endure in our nation's schools before everybody gets on the same page and devises ways to react to emergency situations? Our schools constantly practice fire drills. In fact, Connecticut law dictates that schools practice fire drills on a monthly basis. Yet how many school fires have you seen, heard, or read about? To ignore the possibility of a crisis situation and not implement some kind of response is beyond irresponsible.

Schools should be practicing crisis drills as well as fire drills. Quick—do you know how your local school would react if a gunman entered the building? How about if a plane crashed into the school? (That would never happen, right?) What if a bomb went off?

Yes, I realize in the grand scheme of things that these types of incidents are extremely remote, but you'd have had the same reaction if I predicted in the past that one day the Twin Towers would be felled. A crisis plan is absolutely necessary to anyone involved in a school setting. Teachers need to be made aware of how a certain situation will be handled. They need to know when and where to move the students should an emergency occur.

When a new SRO enters a school, the first thing he should do is make sure that a critical incident plan is in place. If the school already has one, it should be reviewed and deemed applicable. Edits should be made where necessary. If the school does not have a plan in place, then the SRO has a new priority. Above all else, before any other project or investigation is begun, the SRO must work with the school administrators to draft some type of crisis plan on the unfortunate—but possible—chance that an emergency will occur.

Here's one final bit of advice regarding crisis plans. If you're an SRO assigned to a school, and the administrator refuses to have a crisis plan in place...get out of that school! The last thing you need is to be involved with a school administrator who is basically inviting disaster.

Summer

You've heard the comments, I'm sure. Heck, you probably even said it yourself at one point in your life. I know I did: "Teachers are so lucky. They have the summers off." Just make sure you never say that to a teacher.

I learned quickly when I married a teacher (prior to becoming an SRO) that they deserve to have the summers off from work. I'd always see my wife working on lesson plans at night, preparing for the next day. Or she'd be correcting papers and thinking of new ideas to use in the classroom.

Then I became an SRO and saw the abuse teachers take from students who have no respect whatsoever. I saw teachers put up with so much craziness from students, yet have so little power to do anything about it, that I didn't know why anyone would want to become a teacher.

But whether you agree with the practice or not, summers off for our teachers is a nice perk to have.

School resource officers are not teachers. Thus, they do not have summers off. And I'm not going to argue that they should (but a man can dream).

Many police departments across the country utilize their officers in different ways when school is out of session. When I meet an SRO for the first time, one of the first things I ask him or her is what they do in the summertime. The answers I get are various.

One answer does, however, stand out more than any other. Most SROs have told me that their department relegates them back to patrol for the summer months and other school holidays. This also happens to be the path that my department has chosen.

There is nothing wrong with using an SRO for patrol when school is not in session. However, a little common sense should be used. I am well aware that the top administrators in a police department need to worry about budget constraints and overtime issues. But I think they also have a responsibility to look after their workers. Many SROs I've talked to are immediately sent to work second shift patrol (1600-2400 hours) the day after school ends, and they stay on that shift for the rest of the summer. Then they are assigned that same patrol duty each summer. Now any police officer who knows anything will easily agree that the busiest time for a police officer is second shift during the summer months. To take a school resource officer—who deals with many of the same strains that teachers and school officials deal with—and reward him with an annual appointment to the busiest shift during the busiest time of year is an invitation to excessive stress.

The SRO program is still relatively new to many police departments and many officers and police administrators are unaware of the workload that can emerge from a school. This is evident from the constant jabs brother officers give to SROs and the uninformed decisions that some commanding officers make regarding the SRO program. This aforementioned workload coupled with an annual, busy, summer tour of duty will only wear down the average SRO.

Now I'm not saying that SROs should never be sent back to patrol during summer months. In fact, I think it's important that a school resource officer stay acquainted with the duties of patrol work. Many times new patrol techniques are introduced or new forms are used for processing. It's vital that an SRO remain familiar with patrol in case he is reassigned or needed for additional manpower.

This does not mean, however, that the SRO should constantly be assigned the worst of patrol on an annual basis. Even most regular patrolmen have schedules and shifts that vary from year to year so that they do not end up working the same shifts and months year in and year out. Such staggering shift rotation also makes it fair so that the same officers are not always working Christmas Day or Thanksgiving each year.

So for an SRO, or any other officer for that matter, to be assigned the most stressful shift during the summer each and every year is just wrong.

Several police departments realize this and assign their SROs to different types of duties for the summer. Some agencies rotate the SRO's patrol shift each year. For example, during Year A, the SRO is assigned day shift (0800-1600 hours) for the summer months. In Year B, he is assigned to second shift. And for the third year, the SRO would work the midnight shift.

Yet other departments assign their SROs to specialized tasks. Some school resource officers work traffic detail during the summer months either running radar, investigating motor vehicle accidents, or simply doing selective motor vehicle law enforcement.

Other police departments and cities realize that continued contact and integration with the youth in the community is vital to keeping children and teens out of trouble in the summer months. For example, another city in the state of Connecticut—Stamford—implemented a program for its SROs and youth that is so progressive that I believe more cities will follow suit. The description of the program can be found at the following web address:
http://www.usmayors.org/USCM/us_mayor_newspaper/documents/10_09_00/stamford.htm.

I've also included the article here for you to read:

> More than three hundred Stamford middle school students participated in basketball, swimming, computer labs and field trips at camp this past summer in a successful community policing effort that partners a nonprofit community group with the Stamford Police Department and enjoys the strong support of Stamford (CT) Mayor Dannel P Malloy. In its second year of operation, attendance tripled at the summer camp and is expected to keep growing.
>
> "I'm extremely proud of this endeavor," Mayor Malloy said. "I suspect it will be replicated nationally."
>
> The camp is known as an S.R.O. Camp, for school resource officers who during the year are assigned by the police department to Stamford public schools. The relationships the officers build with the students during the year are maintained during the summer months at camp where officers act as referees, umpires and coaches. Camp begins at

noon each day after summer school classes and runs until 5 p.m. and is available to Stamford students entering grades 7 through 9.

"It's fun. We play a lot of sports like basketball and dodge ball and take trips," said one 13-year-old. In addition, there are also games, arts and crafts, talent shows, swim trips to local pools and cookouts. Last summer, students had fun riding on a clipper ship, according to Cindy Morris of the Domus Foundation. "And our mayor [Malloy] here is very wonderful. He's extremely involved with the young people of Stamford and supportive. We love him."

The camp connects community-based organizations with government agencies and private companies. Police Chief Dean Esserman noted that "much of the camp's funding comes from assets seized in drug related crimes" and that the best way to fight crime is to invest in kids. "In my heart, I believe this is police work. To see police as simply and only enforcers of the law is really to miss the point," said Esserman.

The camp, which will be in its third year next summer, was planned by the city's Board of Education, Police Department, the Mayor's Youth Services Bureau and the Domus Foundation. Because of its successful growth, the camp moved from its first year middle school location to Westhill High School, which has an indoor pool, large gymnasium, ball fields, and classrooms available for computer instruction.

The camp is free of charge and open to all Stamford middle school students. In a letter to parents, Mayor Malloy, Chief Esserman, Domus Executive Director Michael Duggan, and Superintendent of Schools Anthony Mazzullo said the SRO Community Camp "will provide a fun, educational and safe summer place where children can work together to create an environment in which respect, self-esteem and teamwork are the basics."

This article is part of The U.S. Conference of Mayors Institute for Community Policing program, funded by the U.S. Department of Justice Office of Community Oriented Policing.

The Stamford model is not only innovative, but necessary as well. As an SRO, I constantly saw adolescents who lacked the social skills needed to become amicable, productive citizens. Too often I saw students who had a neglectful family life. Many students lived only with their mother and had no idea where or who their father was. Some students weren't even that fortunate. Many stayed with grandparents, aunts, uncles, or any relative that would take them. Others were forced into foster homes. These types of family situations have adverse effects on youths. These negative effects are then transferred to the school and social settings.

The Stamford SRO summer program goal is to provide local youths with the activities, discipline, and friendship that they need all while keeping them out of trouble. These types of programs are needed on a much larger level. Other departments within the city should also be providing some kinds of summer programs to keep local youths occupied. The local Boy's Club and YMCA should not be the only places where youngsters can turn. Having SROs provide summer activities to students that they already know, while at the same time teaching them valuable social skills cannot be seen as a waste of police manpower. But that's exactly how other officers view it.

One of my police department's most hotly contested union meetings occurred when the subject of an SRO summer camp came to the floor. The majority of officers were vehemently opposed to the idea. They felt that the SROs should not be allowed to partake in a camp during the summertime while patrolmen were busting their humps answering calls. They felt that they were short-staffed as it was and that the SROs would be better utilized on the street responding to calls.

I found it difficult to challenge that argument. In fact, if I were a patrolman and not an SRO, I would probably have voted down the measure, too. Nevertheless, the fact remains that many school students have nothing to do over the summer and some even get into trouble. These same officers who voted down the SRO summer camp would have to deal with the students who committed criminal acts because they had nothing better to do.

No doubt many other police departments face the same controversy. Should SROs be allowed to hold a summer camp for youths who need structure and activity, or would the department benefit more from their presence on the street? Regardless of who runs it, the camp should be held for the benefit of the youths. Even if the SROs are not the ones to lead it, so be it. A summer activity that teaches discipline, friendship, and fun is needed to stem the current tide of juvenile delinquency. If patrolmen feel that it is unfair for an SRO to be involved with the camp, perhaps private citizens could volunteer or even be hired on a part-time basis to oversee the camp. Maybe even other officers could take turns running the camp. Whatever the decision, a youth summer camp sponsored by the police department and board of education is just another way to take steps to help those youths who, if not involved with the camp, would possibly become entangled in criminal activity. The city of Stamford recognizes this and should be commended for its dedication to the city's youth. Only those who work inside public schools know just how serious some student problems are. Any assistance that governing bodies or municipal departments can give to curb the juvenile and youth problems should be welcomed with open arms. If the youths are not dealt with now in a positive and proactive manner, then the police department will deal with them in a negative, reactive manner when they become adults.

SUMMER

*   *   *

Summertime brings about another issue that a school resource officer has to contend with—graduation.

Throughout my time assigned to Platt High School I have made more friends than I ever thought possible. Not only were the teachers great, but I also became friends with many of the students. At the end of my first year at Platt High School, I realized that I would not see many of the seniors again for quite a long time, if ever. Most headed off to college; some even moved permanently out of state. Still others joined the armed forces—God bless them.

As corny as it sounds, I became attached to many of these students and was sad to see them leave. Now don't get me wrong. There were a few troublemakers whom I held the door open for when they left the building. But just as in society, most of the students are great kids who do a lot of maturing over their four-year stay in high school.

Sometimes, students who had graduated came back to visit. It was amazing to see those former students who became adults. And the best part of their visit was when they smiled at me and told me that they were glad to see me. It made me happy to know that all those years of rapport building and making friends and talking with them had paid off.

For those students who decided not to attend college, or those who commuted to a nearby one, I usually ended up spotting them walking or driving around town. Each year the amount of people I knew and recognized increased as a result of the graduating class that became a full-fledged member of society. It makes me content knowing that each year I knew more and more people in the city of

Meriden that I may one day need to call upon for assistance or who may request my services.

NEW FACES

The 2003/2004 school year was a significant one for me, mostly due to the fact that I was working with several new people. My two main colleagues, Assistant Principals Greg Shugrue and Joeseph Paluszewski had left Platt High School. Shugrue had accepted the position of head principal across town at Maloney High School. Paluszewski had finally called it quits after thirty-five years and decided to retire. Both changes took effect on July 1, 2003.

I had known for some time that Greg and Joe would be leaving, but I didn't expect that time to come so quickly. I wondered to myself, "Who would be their replacements," and, "Am I going to get along with these two new administrators?"

I got my answer in the fall of 2003. Donna Mik and Robert Montemurro were selected as the new assistant principals. This was great news for me because I had known both Rob and Donna during the past few years since they were teachers at Platt High School.

Rob had good administrative experience because he would always fill in for Greg Shugrue whenever Greg was out. In fact, I found Greg and Rob to be very similar, which led to an extremely smooth transition when Greg left.

Donna also proved to be a fine administrator. She never made any drastic changes and she learned her new role quickly and confidently. Both Rob and Donna were a pleasure to work with and they both knew how to utilize me. I was glad to again be working with competent and knowledgeable administrators.

For the months leading up to the selection of new assistant principals, I was a little wary. After all, I didn't know what kind of personalities I was going to end up working with for the coming school year. Were the new assistant principals going to be too inexperienced? Would they have good personalities for the job? How about their work ethic? I know I sound like a member of a board of education preparing for an interview, but these are all relevant questions when it comes to dealing with a school administrator. When I think about it, though, my main concern was that the new administrators might come in and change things for the worse. Luckily for me, the two new assistants proved to be a perfect fit.

A change in personnel can be difficult on an SRO. After several years of getting to know an administrator and knowing what he expects from you and how he's going to handle a situation, an SRO cannot help but become concerned when a new administrator is selected as a replacement. And even though the impending arrival of new assistant principals can be apprehensive to an SRO, it's still not as fretful as getting a new principal. With assistant principals, even if they were to bring any type of change to the school climate, it would be tempered by the fact that the principal is still in charge and his philosophy would dominate.

However, the replacement of a head principal can dramatically alter a school's atmosphere. What if a principal who supported the SRO program was replaced by a principal who didn't? What if a strict principal was replaced by a lenient one? Or vice-versa? To a school resource officer, these are pertinent issues. A principal can make or break the SRO program.

Officer Sal Nesci started at Maloney High School with a principal who was dead set against having an SRO. She soon had a change of heart and eventually became a proponent of the program. When she retired, Greg Shugrue took over. Greg was an even more ardent SRO supporter than his predecessor. Officer Nesci has seen the full circle of principal reaction to the SRO program.

* * *

I've mentioned principals and assistant principals. Is there any other position in the school system that can have an effect on an SRO? How about the superintendent of schools? He might have a little to say about the subject.

As I mentioned earlier in the book, when I first became an SRO the superintendent at the time was not very welcoming to the program. She did not want us to stay in the building and she would not allow us to have offices in her schools, even when the principals requested one for us. Frankly, it was sad.

Fast-forward again to the summer of 2003. The city of Meriden, Connecticut, appoints a new superintendent of schools after the former one retires. And immediately common sense ensues.

I was given an office at the beginning of the 2003/2004 school year. This may have been the single most significant decision by the school since my appointment there. Almost immediately I noticed an increased efficiency in my job performance. I no longer had to run around to find a place to write my reports. Nor did I have to hunt for an available, private phone. I could now make confidential calls from the comfort of my office.

Students, too, could now track me down much more easily. Within days of moving into my office, students became aware of it and walked in to visit with me or talk to me about their concerns. I can honestly say that a day did not go by when someone didn't pay me a visit.

With my new office, I had all my police paperwork separated by labels in my file cabinet. I also had a computer with a printer, as well as access to the Internet. My new office had definitely added much more professionalism to the SRO position and made it that much more of a success.

It truly is amazing how one person can have so much influence. With the appointment of a new superintendent, I went from inefficiency and no office, to professionalism and a place to call my own where students could come to me with their concerns at any time. Even though I knew all along what I needed (as did the principals), the original superintendent—who didn't even know what I did during the day—could not get past the "negative" connotations of housing a police officer in the school. Everyone else, such as parents, students, and school staff members, knew that it only made sense to have my own room, and thankfully the new school superintendent realized this as well.

The bottom line is that those SROs who are not afforded the luxury of an office should not give up hope. (Remember, it took me three years!) Your school administrators may be too busy with other important matters than to focus on police problems such as office space. But if and when that day finally comes when you are given a place of your own, not only will you be satisfied, but the whole school will benefit as well.

*　　　　　*　　　　　*

This chapter deals with new faces, new personnel. And I need to focus on another group of people that may transfer, retire, etc., who have an impact on your position: other SROs.

When Officer Kristin Muir left Lincoln Middle School to have a baby, the search was on for a new officer to take her place. Once again, not many officers showed interest in the position because they didn't want to deal with kids and the school environment. Since I was going to be working closely with the new chosen officer, I became very concerned with who might be selected. Thankfully, my department made an excellent choice in Officer Steve Lespier.

Steve and I continued what Kristin and I began. And it was a seamless transition. Steve had the flexible personality needed to maintain a successful SRO program. He knew how to interact with middle-school kids on a level that they could appreciate. But at the same time, he knew how to be stern when need be. I was very happy with the selection.

Many SROs will not have to worry about the selection of a new school resource officer. Some school districts only have one officer, while others have four in one school! For those departments that have several SROs, it is important to get a group of officers that get along with each other and share the same work ethic. If one of the SROs in the group is not pulling his weight in his respective school, it could easily have a negative impact on the whole unit.

Besides your fellow SROs, another important position is the school resource officer supervisor. It only makes sense for a supervisor well versed in juvenile law and community policing to head the SRO unit.

During a transitional phase in my department, there was a period of eight months where the SROs went through five different supervisors. This can be very distracting and frustrating as every supervisor has his own vision for the program and at times can contradict his predecessor's goals.

Some supervisors with no experience in the SRO field also believe that the position is a joke (as do many patrolman). But this belief comes from not knowing enough about the duties an SRO performs. To be fair, many supervisors and fellow officers appreciate the program because they know it saves them time from many school-related investigations. In any event, I have found that a successful SRO supervisor should have knowledge of juvenile law, an excellent demeanor for dealing with school officials and parents of students, familiarity with the program, and a general idea of how to keep the SRO program running in a positive direction.

To be sure, a school district that exhibits an SRO-friendly superintendent, school administration, and police force will find it virtually impossible for the program to fail.

Maintaining the Program

Everything I've described in this book occurred during my first four years at the high school. You'd think that after all that time I'd get burned out or disinterested with the SRO program.

On the contrary.

I can honestly say that each successive year only got better for me. Each new school year enabled me to meet new students. Also, I became so close with faculty members that I really couldn't picture myself ever not working with them. I felt in control of my position. Students knew what to expect from me, and they knew what I expected from them. I became very comfortable and knowledgeable regarding my position as SRO and, as such, I continued to strive for new and innovative ways to improve the program. What follows are several ideas I implemented in order to continue the positive SRO experience.

During my first year at the school, I was driving home one day in December when I heard on the radio that some organization (it may have even been the state police—I can't recall) was sponsoring a "Stuff-A-Bus" campaign. Area residents were asked to bring toys to the bus and fill it up so that the toys could be donated to needy children. A great idea, I thought. So great, that I decided to borrow it and use my police cruiser to hold a "Stuff-A-Cruiser" campaign for Christmas. I got together with one of the school's social clubs called The Interact Club. This club was sponsored by Meriden's Rotary Club and the students who comprise it work with various charitable groups and hold fund-raisers. The teacher in charge of the club—as well as the students themselves—loved the idea.

The "Stuff-A-Cruiser" campaign was so successful that The Interact Club and I actually won a state educational award for it and brought a plaque back to the school. Every year thereafter, the Interact Club and I held the "Stuff-A-Cruiser" event one week before Christmas. It became a tradition at the school. We collected the toys in the cruiser, then we drove down to children's and nursing homes and dispersed the toys and gifts while the members of the club sang carols.

After the first year, my cruiser was no longer big enough to hold all the toys. Officer Kristin Muir had helped me in the past by bringing her cruiser to contain the overflow, and then Officer Steve Lespier (her replacement) assisted me in the years to since.

The "Stuff-A-Cruiser" campaign was a fun, holiday event But it only happened once a year. During my second year at the school, I began to think of how I could help students learn more about the policing experience while at the same time forming an even stronger bond with them. The result: RAPP.

RAPP stands for Ride-Along Police Program. The Meriden Police Department has a civilian ride-along program for those interested. In fact, that is how I became initiated in the police world. Before becoming an officer, I rode with a patrolman via the civilian ride-along program. He showed me the many aspects of police work and the rest was history.

I decided that I would give interested Platt High School students the same opportunity. Making sure to first clear it with the principal and my supervisor, I decided that RAPP would consist of a one-hour ride-along with a student and me. School ended at 1:53 p.m., so I would hold the session from 2:00 p.m. to 3:00 p.m. Together the student and I would go to nearby calls for service, perform motor vehicle stops, and run radar. After our one-hour tour of duty ended, I would drop the student off at his house.

When I initially started RAPP, I hung fliers in the school hallways and advertised the program. I left a sign-up sheet in the main office and hoped to get at least ten signatures. Within a week I had fifty sign-ups. I was floored. Each student who signed up was given a permission slip that had to be signed by a parent. I also made sure to call the parent after I received the slip to verify that it was their signature. Once everything was signed and agreed upon, the student and I went on our one-hour tour.

I began RAPP in January 2002, and it continued for the rest of the school year. It was much more work than I thought. Because of it, I had to cancel many other after school obligations such as meetings with parents or teachers, and I would frequently have to postpone my paperwork until the morning. Also, the permission slips were a slight hassle because not only did the parent and student have to sign it, but each day I had to track down the lieutenant from the day patrol shift and have him sign it as well.

Even though there were a few minor glitches (what inaugural program doesn't have them) RAPP was an enormous success. Students got to see real police work in action. They asked many questions and learned things about law enforcement that they previously never knew. Some students who showed no emotion in school had their faces light up when I asked them to turn the siren on. Many students asked if they could ride with me again. In fact, many students still came up to me after I suspended the program and asked when I was going to start RAPP again. They were very eager to ride along, especially after hearing all the positive feedback from those who had already experienced it.

Making RAPP available throughout the entire school year would mean having to put other duties on hold. By offering RAPP from January through June, I was able to take care of other matters at the beginning of the year and make room for the ride-alongs in the latter half of the school year.

Besides giving the student a lesson in law enforcement, RAPP enabled me to get to know the student better. It gave the two of us a chance to chitchat and talk about the school we both attended. This type of close communication between officer and student would be unheard of were it not for the School Resource Officer program which builds trust and friendship between police and America's future.

Another way that I thought I could keep in touch with the student body was through the high school newspaper. Platt's student newspaper was run by the students, for the students. I thought it would be a good idea for me to write a column in each edition of the newspaper so that I could communicate with them in yet another fashion. I knew I'd have to ask the student editor's if they thought my own column would be a good idea. I definitely would not want to do it if the newspaper staff was opposed to the idea. I spoke with the editor and the teacher who oversaw the production of the paper. They said they thought it would be a great idea and would bring it up in the next meeting. Within a few days, the editor got back to me and said the staff would love to print my column. I was very pleased to hear their positive reaction and immediately began my foray into the school newspaper as an SRO.

Officer Sal Nesci devised his own project across town at Maloney High School. He got together with interested students at his school and sponsored a Safe Halloween Trick-or-Treat at the school. Combined with candy donations from local businesses, Nesci and the students set up the school's hallways on Halloween night to offer a safe alternative for youngsters to come with their families and trick-or-treat. The project was an enormous success. All of Meriden's SROs were present and we were amazed at the turnout. Nesci's project even ended up on the local evening news.

Ideas such as these are what keep an SRO program running. As an SRO, you should try to do whatever it takes to develop a positive relationship with the students and faculty. If you're a school resource officer, please feel free to use any of the above ideas. They've been enormously successful for me and I'm sure they would thrive in many schools.

The key to a prosperous, lasting SRO program is to constantly try new ideas. Don't enter a school and stagnate. Constantly strive to invigorate yourself as well as the students. Just as in any aspect of society, time forces us to change with it. Imagine police forces using the same investigative techniques now as they did twenty years ago. Imagine teachers using thirty-year-old educational methods in today's classroom. It would be an invitation for failure. The SRO program must abide by the same rule. The program should grow with the times.

A school resource officer who does not attempt to make his program successful will have a tough time. Students are very intuitive and will be able to see that the officer does not really care about what he is doing. And if the students begin to think that their SRO doesn't care about them...then they won't care about their SRO, and the program will be for naught.

* * *

So there you have it. The life and times of a school resource officer. When I joined the police force in 1996 I never would've dreamed that one day I'd be stationed at a public high school. But now it is easy to envision. I've gained a whole new slew of friends in the teachers and students that I've met. I was part of a specialized group of law enforcement officers who (hopefully) make some kind of positive impact on the students they serve. And the position is still a relatively new one. SROs are constantly being added to schools each year. Some people are still not aware of what an SRO is. I always used to introduce myself as a "school resource officer" and not an "SRO" because many people don't know what "SRO" stands for. Single Room Occupancy? Standing Room Only? It's not a household acronym yet.

I am confident, however, that the SRO position will become quite common in the future. In fact, I can foresee a time when a school is looked down upon for not having an SRO. And why wouldn't a board of education add an SRO to its system? Ever since the program began in Meriden, I can't recall any negative feedback about it. Parents seem to love it. School staff welcome it. And most students are satisfied with it. Obviously those students who are used to breaking school rules and even criminal law in the building probably wish the SRO wasn't there. But even they end up usually needing his service at one time or another.

The SRO position is such a unique one. It combines the authority of law enforcement with the educational aspects of teaching. It gives police officers a whole new way to interact with children and teenagers in a positive light, instead of constantly being viewed as "hard-nosed" and "unfeeling." When looking at all the positive aspects of the SRO program, only one question seems to stand out: why wasn't this program implemented earlier?

Truth be told, it wasn't too long ago that police were not welcome on school campuses. It was believed that the school setting was not a place for a police officer. If in the unusual event that police response was needed, a plain clothes detective was sent over so as not to raise any fears or concerns. Again, this type of behavior only increased the chasm between police and community relations. It fed into the belief that the police should only be called for very bad situations.

But citizens, parents, and school boards only begin to sit up and take notice when shootings start erupting in schools. Columbine. Paducah. Jonesboro. Santee. Why is it that only after these terrible tragedies were police asked to join schools across the country? Why do people think that a school is dangerous and unsafe when they see an SRO assigned there? If anything, isn't the school much safer?

Instead of understanding the goal of the SRO program—to integrate police with youths to form a better bond between law enforcement and society's future—some people automatically assume the worst because they themselves cannot get past the police stereotype. It is only with the continued dedication of hardworking school resource officers—along with support from the school community—that people will begin to better understand the role of the SRO.

Index

C

Cheshire Police Department 112
corporal punishment 88
Criminal Investigation 42

D

D.A.R.E. 9
Die Hard 62
Direct Connect 147
Don Kings 78, 79

F

Fourth Amendment 89

G

Gaffney, Tim 51, 119

H

Holland, Danny 71

I

In re: D.E.M. v. Commonwealth of Pennsylvania 93
informants .. 42, 43, 46, 47, 73, 76, 91, 136
Ingala, Trooper Heather ... 52, 148
Interact Club, The 171

J

James, Dr. Bernard 91, 97

K

Kids & Khemicals 71
Killing Mr. Griffin 70

L

Labas, Gladys 120
Lane, Officer Mike 9, 67, 77, 119, 151
legitimate informers 43, 46
Lespier, Officer Steve 47, 167
Lethal Weapon 62
Lincoln Middle School 9, 10, 29, 64, 67, 147, 150, 167

M

Maloney High School 105
Meriden 1
Meriden Police Department ... iii, 1, 10, 47, 54, 71, 72, 121, 172
Mik, Donna 163
modified-Weaver stance 63
Montemurro, Robert 163
Muir, Officer Kristin 8, 10, 29, 64, 76, 147, 167, 171

N

NASRO 13
National Association of School Resource Officers .... *See* NASRO
Nesci, Officer Sal ... 9, 36, 76, 105, 120, 145, 165, 174
New Jersey v. T.L.O. 90
Nextel 146

O

Operation Sidewalk 65

P

Paluszewski, Joseph... 40, 125
Parent & Teen Universities, Inc. 72
Platt High School....4, 5, 7, 9, 17, 18, 25, 26, 40, 45, 46, 47, 50, 54, 61, 64, 75, 78, 79, 81, 82, 84, 87, 97, 100, 101, 105, 106, 119, 125, 126, 130, 137, 143, 145, 146, 150, 161, 163, 164, 172
police mountain bike 149

R

RAPP *See* Ride-Along Police Program
reasonable suspicion 90
Ride-Along Police Program 172

S

Safe Halloween Trick-or-Treat 174
School COP 82
self-aggrandizing informants 43, 46
Shugrue, Greg...39, 125, 163, 164, 165

Sig Sauer 58
Smith, Tom 70
South Vine St 64
Southington Police Department 61
Southington Public High School 60
State of Wisconsin v. Angelia D.B. 92
student mediation 77
Stuff-A-Cruiser 171

T

Thorp, Lt. John 4, 11, 70, 122
TRIAD 13
Triano, Officer Gerry 60
Trosell, Peter 70

V

Vitale, Officer Joe 112

W

Washington Middle School 119
Wilson, Marty 115
Wisconsin Supreme Court . 92
www.p-t-u.org 72

Z

zero-tolerance 80